# The Crack in a Voice

# The Crack in a Voice

## A Memoir in Verse

Doug Jennette

WILLOWSONG PRESS

RALEIGH, NORTH CAROLINA

**WillowSong Press**
618 Stacy Street
Raleigh, North Carolina  27607

The Crack in a Voice: A Memoir in Verse / Douglas Jennette — 1st ed.
ISBN  978-0-578-81440-7

The Crack in a Voice: A Memoir in Verse / Douglas Jennette — E-Pub
ISBN  978-0-578-81441-4

*Cover and author photographs by Marsha Presnell-Jennette*

*Design and publishing services by Carol Majors*
Publications Unltd • Raleigh NC

To my mother, Alice Deans Jennette,
who taught me the value of reading
and of listening to the imagination
and the wealth
of beauty and inspiration
to be found in the natural world.

To my wife, Marsha Anne Presnell-Jennette,
who taught me to take notice and celebrate life
in the seen and unseen world around us.
She teaches me each day about friendship,
determination, beauty, and the magic
that makes life miraculous.
For this, I am eternally grateful.

~

*"Poetry is language against which you have no defenses."*

DAVID WHYTE

# Contents

"*What does it mean, then, to love one's country, and what does it mean to be a patriot? If a poet is busy all his life fighting prejudices, removing narrow views, enlightening the mind of his people, purifying their taste, and ennobling their opinions and thoughts, how could he do better or be more patriotic?*"

J. W. von Goethe

# Preface

I come from a long line of eastern North Carolina farmers, who never accumulated much money or property, but prided themselves on their self-sufficiency. The rural area which was my home until my eighth birthday was near my paternal grandparents, but was remote from peers and the activities that small-town America offered in the 1950s. My parents' move to small-town Garner, NC in December 1955 was a pivotal point in their lives and that of our family. It allowed my father some distance from the drudgery of farming and events surrounding his involuntary psychiatric hospital admissions, my parents a measure of freedom from family entanglements, and allowed my sister and me the opportunity to grow up among other children and families different from ours. I will always be grateful to them for that decision.

The poems in this book span many decades and most of the developmental phases in my life thus far. They began to appear in the late 1960s in response to the upheaval around the Vietnam War, civil rights, and my growing relationship with my future wife, Marsha. Poems from that time reflect intense emotions and imagery and grew out of a somewhat solitary and depressed early college experience. As with most of my work, they were "inspirational" — meaning they were inspired by an image, phrase, emotion, or longing and flowed out without much editing or crafting involved. As presented here, these "Early Times" poems are in the state they were in when I left them following my graduation from college in 1970.

The 1970s and much of the 1980s were poetically quiet for me, with only an occasional reading of others' poetry to remind me of the power in that form. Life's energy and focus were on creating a good marriage, learning how to become a competent clinical social worker, and redefining/expanding my spiritual life through the practice of Quakerism. Reading Alexander Solzhenitsyn's harrowing accounts of life in the Soviet gulag system gave me an invaluable perspective on the capacity of human beings to inflict horrors on others in the name of political goals. Occasional letters to the Editor of our local newspaper helped exercise and focus my writing skills.

The late 1980s began the next phase of my creativity, largely spurred by a desire to discover, define, and enhance my sense of myself as a man by developing meaningful connections with other men. My involvement in the Mythopoetic branch of the Men's Movement was the vehicle for this journey. Robert Bly, poet and men's conference leader, was both inspirational and invitational — he inspired me to pay attention to my life as a man and invited a creative response from which poems again began to flow.

Attending men's retreats, getting to know, value and find deep affection for other men, and working with other men to create the Raleigh Men's Center (now The Men's Council) supported the re-emergence of my poetic expression. Poems from this period are reflective and attuned to the details of life, nature, and relationships. And they honor, both directly and indirectly, the men who helped me soften what Bruce Springsteen calls "the pathological urge toward isolation" that is a specter in the lives of many men.

It has been noted that many of my poems carry a sense of loss, grief, or wistful melancholy. I think this is in part due to my nature and in part due to my understanding that, particularly for men, being able to recognize, acknowledge, and express grief is a healthy skill and a sometime antidote to depression. Robert Bly articulated this premise, and I have found it to be true in my life.

The next phase of my poetry began in early 2010 when a friend, Ed Lyons, offered to play music with me as a Christmas gift. I had been away from my guitar for many years and found the offer immediately appealing. Ed is a talented multi-instrumentalist who composes and arranges music. Quickly, song lyrics began to flow whose themes can be generally described as "country." Again, these lyrics were inspired by an off-hand phrase, image, or concept — usually relating to some aspect of the relationship between women and men. My rusty and rudimentary guitar skills meant that the songs developed as stories, rather than musical compositions. This period produced several completed songs and some worthy fragments.

Interestingly, another musician friend, Chris Royce who, like Ed, is a gifted guitarist and composer, provided my next nudge into lyric composition. Chris was my guitar teacher for a time in the early 1980s, and we had remained friends over the years. I retired at the end of 2018, and Chris invited me to write lyrics for a couple of his compositions in early 2019. Thus began a fun and fruitful collaboration that continues to the present. Chris has composed music to some of my lyrics and, most gratifyingly, set the poem "Shadowman" to a full arrangement with acoustic and slide guitar, bass, banjo, percussion, and clarinet. Chris plays all the stringed instruments. Shadowman can be found as a music video on his website at *bigwoodsmusic.com.*

The decision to write a brief introduction to all but the earliest poems means this book has a "memoir-ish" quality — offering context to locate the poems in time, place and life phase. Clearly, poems I've written in recent years are influenced by the decline and death of my parents and dear friends, increasing awareness of my own mortality, especially in conversations with my men's group (we have met twice monthly for 31 years), and retirement from my work spanning nearly 50 years as a clinical social worker.

As I was putting the finishing touches on this book in early 2020, I could not foresee the Covid-19 pandemic and did not anticipate the coinciding social upheaval in the US and elsewhere against systemic racism and the persistent killing of Black people by police and others. Both these processes remain ongoing, with their ultimate outcomes far from predictable. Apart from three poems, this book reflects almost nothing of these events that will be defining aspects of 2020 and beyond. Only history can determine their significance, but they propel a change and reckoning that has been a long time coming.

Ernest Becker, in the introduction to his 1973 "The Denial of Death," writes about the human "mythical hero-system" in which we strive for a kind of immortality by creating edifices (temples, skyscrapers, books) which provide a sense that we have primary value and worth in the world around us. To the extent that this book is one of my immortality projects, the ultimate worth of it will be determined by the reader. It has been both laborious and delightful to interact with this rather modest body of work, enjoy the memory of the creation of it, make it as good as my creative talents allow, take pleasure in the images and sounds, and offer it to anyone who may be curious about the nearly life-long musings of a retired psychotherapist. ✍

# Acknowledgments

I am indebted to family, friends, and clients who, over the years, inspired, encouraged and modeled how to live decent lives. There have always been more people in my web of affection and support than can adequately be noted here. However, I will single out a few who have been instrumental in my appreciation for and offering of poems to the world in response to the experience of being human.

Poets Larry Sorkin, Lou Lipsitz and Bennett Myers have offered friendship and guidance in ways they may not be fully aware of as we explored our experience as men in search of fellowship, intimacy, open-heartedness and service. They are models of men who work to remain in tune with their creativity and the rewards of friendship.

The poet and writer Robert Bly introduced me to men's work, as well as the poetry of grief and the deep masculine desire for male connection. His flamboyant style was refreshing. Leonard Cohen's capacity for speaking to the dark side of human experience in poetry, song and fiction was both appealing and disarmingly intimate. And his evolution as a man who could still make art from his flaws into his 80's holds out hope for those of us who approach that milestone.

Thanks to my friend and former office mate/colleague Mike Katz, with whom I worked for twenty-eight years — together we created/shared a variety of professional and personal learning experiences. His friendship, wise counsel, insightful perspective and support for my creativity were part of the anchoring structure that enabled my practice of psychotherapy and the creation of this book. I'm grateful to remain part of his loving intentional family.

For over thirty years (and prior to the radical changes in psychotherapy the Covid-19 pandemic has brought), I was fortunate to be part of two peer-supervision groups, one of which I continue to attend for its twice-monthly meeting. Without their professional and personal support/fellowship my career would not have been sustainable. So, thanks to Ann, Tom, Dan and Barbara — I miss our monthly reflections. And to Don, Jean, Pat, Lea and Steve — I look forward to our continued connection, mutual support, and the professional expertise we offer each other as we approach and arrive at retirement.

Douglas Joe Lester was a dear friend who died in 2018. In 1986, we helped found the Raleigh Men's Center (now The Men's Council) and explored men's work together in a variety of ways over the years. His leadership and promotional skills, fierce open-hearted courage, good humor, and love of life were deeply inspiring for me. I'll be forever grateful for the times we had together.

My men's support group began in 1989 with nine psychotherapists and survives with four of us from that original group. I cannot imagine what life would be like without this source of intimacy, humor, support, fellowship and grace as we explore our 70's together. So, to Mike, Richard and Steve — much gratitude for your loving kindnesses and the years we have yet to share.

My sister, Betsy, has been a loving support for my creativity for many years. As a storyteller, painter, writer and poet she brings passion and perceptivity to her roles as mother, teacher, community volunteer and friend. Our shared family history and our capacity to frequently reflect on it together have been deep sources of support and strength for me.

The creation of this book would not have been possible without the technical expertise and project support of Carol Majors. Carol's knowledge of the publishing process, her experience with design, layout, and organization, patience with changes that required re-working the structure of the work, and her editing skills were both necessary and invaluable. Many thanks to Carol.

And, finally, my wife Marsha is my original Muse and my forever companion. Her creativity, enthusiasm, humor, intelligence and love have added immeasurably to my life as a whole and to the work that is reflected here. She is a source of continuing inspiration, without which this book would have remained an aspirational fantasy. Thanks, Sweetie! ✒

# The Human Condition

"This being human is a guest house, each day a new arrival."
RUMI

**Silence**

A simple silent day.
How odd that sounds in a world of
raging machines
instant messaging and a
multitude of unsatisfying choices to
feed a starving soul.

But this silence filled
my soul with
warm connections
common unity (community) and
remembrance of that which is
not passed, but
ever present.

Simple God-felt musings that
held us in our freedom like
lovers seeing the truest self in
each others eyes.

So on it goes into
the next day and the next.
A silence that leaps out, like
dancing fawns with
merry, glistening eyes
sunlight, fog and shadow
newly leafing trees and
irregular light patterns on asphalt,
fairy ponds in a desert.

My soul is bursting with love and
gratitude for the beauty and
banality of my life
and compassion for petty grievances
and tenderly nurtured hurts.

It is moments like these of
truth so fine and rare,
golden threads floating on August breezes,
that tears are the only fitting offering
to this god.
And a thousand "thank you's" spoken
and not, into
and out of that cool, clear
well of silence. ✒

**The Crack in a Voice**

What leaks out through the crack
in a voice?
Is it all of humanity or the cry of a hungry bluebird
with one blind eye?

Perhaps the man from Georgia says it best
"I bought a guitar instead
of an engagement ring
and it fucked up the whole deal
for thirty two years."
Raw, slow, real
like coarse sandpaper on heart pine
owning life's mistake while
wishing it were not so.

The dear man from Minnesota shows
grief and gratitude for his father
the only man in his county to read books
during the Great Depression-
a father who gave his boy permission to
write books of poetry out of his own sorrow.
Face flush, eyes welling and overflowing like
dew forming on medieval stained glass windows
weariness resting on the landscape of his face
sinuses congesting with the ache of recognition and remembrance
this man honors his father, himself and us
by letting the crack widen to allow in ninety men
while forever holding a mirror to our souls.

Here stands the fighter, a father five times over who knows loss
but never gives up
and wears his passion on his sleeve.

He sells his dreams one man at a time,
ripe yellow melons in an Eastern market
and loves the men who taste them for a moment.
He goes on wanting that passion to live in a wider circle
afraid of its passing too soon,
like the glint of light from golden tail feathers of some great bird
flying too low to the ground at dusk.
The grief may go un-noticed unless
his voice is heard
by one who walks shoulder to shoulder
fear to fear through the years
following his lead.
The fighter, sensing defeat, stops for a moment to gather himself
    chest to chest
and the crack widens to let in love.
And he is gone.

The ex-professor, on a colorful April day, speaks
in poetry of his father
a man who loved the ballgame of life
enough to gamble recklessly and well
in this garden of earthly delights.
A jagged crack in his voice unexpectedly appears
and we are there to witness and feel and know
a measure of this man's love for his gambler
and his courage to be known
a sacrifice for us all to the god of shame
whom we worship in secret and in silence.

Another man, an academic, Jungian intellectual
straight as a sixty foot poplar
impeccable in his control

reads of a poet frantically running through an airport to
be with her dying father.
A crack in his voice echoes off the sparking
stream from his left eye.
And we are here with this man
and woman and anyone whose father may leave
before the last goodbye.
Reading through the feeling, small gasps to catch his
breath, a child afraid of losing his way
this man holds on with courage through a storm of emotion
lighting the path for others.

And what of me?
What leaks out through the crack in my voice?
These images linger in my heart
twilight shadows
offering the familiarity of smooth, round stones and
the smell of woodsmoke in winter.
Like these men, do I breathe in deeply to let out all of my humanity?
Or do I chirp like the blue iridescence of feather and bone with the
cloudy left eye?

Today, I do not know but think
maybe I move in a great arc
following some inner stars
half blind and afraid, but alert
to signs guiding me downward and
home. ✒

**What Would Rumi Say?**

What would Rumi say, watching half-ton bombs decimate
his culture's place of birth?
Would undulating earth provoke images
of midnight lovemaking and mirth?
Would the crying sky call forth comparisons
with ivory ash or burned leaf skeletons
spiraling on crisp fall breezes?

Would he propose, only half in jest, that those who live underground
are of another race or species
blind, like moles, but highly prized?
Would the pain of this season of destruction be too great
even for one buoyed on the breath of the Beloved?
Would this carnival of terror find meaning
in his hooded stare and be seen, through a silent tear
as the way we break the walls between
this world and the next?

Hate invites a familiar partner to this
rosy dance of death. We will not disappoint
or shyly turn away.

What would Rumi say? ᴊ•

## Time

Is there time
enough
for nothing
to happen?

I ask myself
if I can
patiently wait
while nothing
happens.

Or do I rush to
create something
anything
to soften this
knife-edged silence
in my
heart. ✐

**The Dark**

I shower in the dark
for what is there to see?

Water falling down
on the familiarity
of me.

And returning
to the sea
eventually. ❧

## The Children

Today, I heard an interview with single women
talking wistfully about their sperm donors.
Some admitted their fantasies about this anonymous father-
"You know, tall, dark, handsome, a real stud of Spanish descent"
and images of marriage and trips to Barcelona with moonlight
    strolls.
But most would not want to meet him in life or communicate
even if they could.
"He might be a bum, a jerk or just no good — and then what?"

Some fear of attachment or the loss of a certain hard-won
    independence
seems to claim these well spoken women.
And they laugh and tell their children,
"No, you have no father, just you and me
and our little village."
Then they show photographs of his region or geographic locale
as if these shadows could substitute for him.
A world without mothers would be inconceivable
to these enlightened women.

But what of the children who cry in the night
for fathers they can never know
and rage at mothers too independent and afraid
to risk a helpmate father?
Has it come to this
a sophisticated madness simply because it's possible?

Beware of fatherless children
for their hearts are fearful and
they will not show mercy or restraint.  ⊷

**The Child Grown Old**
 **(or I Ain't as Stupid as Most Folks Think)**

Once more man comes to journey's end
and he never suspects what might have been.
Had he been born with face that's fair
and blond instead of kinky hair.

Had he been told to lift his face
in sun and moon and public place
instead of yes Sir, no Sir, Ma'am
to folks who just don't give a damn.

Had he been shown his inner path
in books of chemistry or math,
or learned the secrets of the mind
in nice front room, not out behind.

Had he been taught delight, not sorrow
had hope for now, not just tomorrow-
been offered more than pie in the sky
with just reward only when you die.

Had someone seen upon his face
that inner fire that has no "place."
Had he been given just half a chance
to learn a poem 'stead of song-and-dance.

Had someone seen this life-long play
and known he knew there's a better way.
Had someone known his name was Roy
and called him that instead of boy.

Had he been tried like me or you

before being told the job was through,
or served up food from counter line
as good or warm as yours or mine.

And just one time had someone smiled
as walking down that lonesome mile
he chanced to pass his fellow man
and tried to talk or lend a hand.

Had folks just realized the fate
of pious arrogance and hate,
they would have said "why, come on in
all men are brothers, cousins, kin."

Now snow's upon that furrowed brow
and other brothers cannot see how
this man can only watch and sit
while in his land (in which he never fit)
right cause is given praise and shout
and law is seen as reason to flout
the upper-crust, the cracker crowd
who's running scared and sweats out loud.

For him it is a little late.
The fire is gone, his path is straight.
A mind unequal to the task
so be it now, but not in the past.

Come look into his closing eyes
and listen for his dying sighs
and try to tell yourself again,
"No, he don't know what might have been." ✒

## Stan

For me, it always been about the melody.
He was a straight-A student
who fell in love with the saxophone at
age 13, enough to quit school to play music until
he was dragged back against his will by truant officers.

He played tenor with the best as a teen
and led his recording sessions
by his early 20's. He idolized Lester
and played with Woody, Dizzy, Oscar, Horace
Byrd and Jobim.

Zoot said he was a nice bunch of guys and
he, like a lot of the bebop and cool jazzmen
found a love of dope landed him in non-music
jams on more than one occasion, before finding sobriety
and serenity toward the end.

Bossa Nova brought him Grammys and worldwide fame.
He followed his heart into lots of others' bedrooms
sometimes with career changing results. But his voice
remained true, asking his horn to pour out all the
fire and ice it could not hold, every time he played.

He toyed with fusion but returned to his roots as the
    20th Century
wound down. Finding that next phrase or color or inflection was
a life-long quest, and his peers had admiration for his artistry
if not always for his manner. He made it to 64, about average for
    his breed
before liver cancer silenced his horn.

So, when I'm feeling up or a little down
I return to the well where Stan Getz left his soul
and let Moonlight in Vermont wash over me
knowing I'll find a melody that makes me smile and
a wispy, mellow tone that breaks my heart every time.

As Duke once said about music, "If it sounds good
it is good." ✍

## Shadowman

I'm a carnival barker in a bright red hat
who can break you down in nothing flat
I'll pull you in and give you what you want.
I'm smooth, I'm harsh, I know the dance
and I can match your pale romance
with images that leave your body taut.

I'm a tightrope walker in a tailored suit
a blond haired beauty who will bend the truth
in ways that bring your family to tears.
I take shapes that keep you up at night
while spinning wildly with delight
they must reflect your meanest, darkest fears.

I'm your priest, your pappa, and your pimp.
I jeer with pleasure at your pitiful limp.
I know your soul and say just what you think.
I read the leaves, I keep the score
and see deep down you thirst for more
than your meager life has given you to drink.

So, come on folks the water's fine.
I have new smart phones and cheap red wine
that call your buried wishes and desires.
Let me do what I want with all those Others
for they are not your sisters or your mothers
just ready targets for the usual liars.

Now hold your nose and dive right in
I'm your school-yard bully and your new best friend
through all the twisted hallways of this chase.
You may be angry, you may be scared

you may lose yourself, but you don't care
you know that I'm your hidden, other face.

I'm the midnight shadow on your bedroom wall
and I know that you will take the fall
when times get worse and your fragile world is sinking.
I've rigged the game and stacked the cards
and now your life is jagged shards
of what was grand, come on, what were you thinking?

I hear a funeral bell, can you hear it? Something's stinking. ✿

*July, 2016*
*With appreciation to Leonard Cohen (1934–2016)*

**Rifle**

The violent fantasies were always heroic
defending friends or family with
the 1936 Remington pump .22
(scoped for distance and accuracy)
once my father's hunting rifle
now mine as a link to him.

Usually it was some faceless threat —
neo-nazis coming for a Jewish friend
or some ill-formed Armageddon scene
me bravely holding off hordes while my wife escaped.
It was never an angry "I'll show them"
random shooting or revenge for real
or imagined injustices. Rarely the idea might float through that if
    my health or life
became unbearable there would be a quick resolution.

I don't know when they started, these
heroic fantasies. Maybe they came before
I acquired the rifle as a middle-aged adult
like the fantasies boys of a certain age
reveled in and acted out with sticks and
pieces of wood with nails for triggers
in woods or back yards or alleys of '50s and '60s America.

I know the difference between fantasy and intent
and could have killed a treasured teenage friend
foolish enough to wake me
past midnight by tapping
on my basement bedroom window.
I don't remember thinking anything, only
in that moment the clear intent to rise

and grab the loaded .12 gage shotgun
a few feet away and
blast the window.
Only the paralysis of my fear saved our lives from tragedy.
You see, our house had loaded hunting guns in plain
    sight — remnants of a rural past
and a time before mass shootings made it mostly unthinkable.

I know when they stopped, these heroic fantasies.
After the carnage at Mother Emanuel that old .22 felt
heavy on my heart, a burden on my soul.
I could not escape the images of those murdered worshipers
bowed and bloody sacrifices to a racist fantasy.
And so, the rifle left my house to be stored in my brother in law's
    gun safe.

And the heroic fantasies left my imagination as well — gone like
    smoke in a fresh breeze.
I find it hard to believe they ever existed. ❧

**Refugee**

Like you, I am a refugee.
Long ago I abandoned a place
to which I can never
return, to face an arduous search
for a welcoming and warm replacement.
I am a refugee.

I stake my tenuous claim here
to this little piece of ground
where I belong and sometimes
feel like a stranger.
I search for kindred souls
with familiar markings
or accents.
I nurture and am nurtured, comfort
and cause pain
all the while holding a deep
and abiding desire to be free
of that earlier place, and
return to it.

Sometimes I carry heavy, tattered clothing
in a canvas satchel
on my back, thin straps painfully
biting into shoulder muscle.
At other times my load is light and buoyant
like gossamer bubbles rising from secret
dark places toward
sunflower light. Tension between the
old and the new is
achingly alive.

Today I come into this sacred place
created by wanderers
and find you here. We have come
as Friends, singly or in pairs, and together
we take our longings
into silence.
The merging of heavy hooves and luminous wings
of deep humanity and unending
spirit often leads to new
awakenings. I bless and
am blessed.

The words we offer
speak of holy and sometimes dangerous
journeys, the meandering path
of the dove
or the bullet trajectory of the
peregrine falcon
all expressions of the soul's hunger
for the landscape and safety
of a familiar
resting place.

I am comforted, alarmed, amused and sometimes
puzzled by our little band and
our divine humanness.
Your spoken words or
intonations find intimate
and tender places within me
like golden threads from our hearts reaching
upward, or a dark
distorting mirror so close as to be
fogged by our
shallow breathing.

You and I may be a long way
from our destinations, or we may have already
fully arrived. Either way, for now, we have
each other.
We will continue our soul searches together
arms reaching out in a great circle
often joyful and at times fearless
yet mindful of the still, small voice
and ever alert to signs, like flickering inner firelight
guiding us onward. ⌇

*for Raleigh Friends Meeting*

## Profanity / The Curse

"Twenty children and six
adults and the shooter
as well as another adult off site." These
disembodied words strike like a fist
behind my ear. Stunning and vivid
and deeply disturbing. Repulsed, I feel compelled
to listen
for more of the bloody details. And this close
to Christmas — just too much to endure for the
families whose lives and holiday are
forever shattered.
That the first victim
was his mother makes it less the work
of a psychotic madman and more a gushing
eruption from a deeply felt wound, according
to the NPR resident expert on mass killings.
What a job!

And just yesterday a Chinaman with his knife, who
bloodied dozens of school children
may have intended death, but for the lack of
firepower failed to rob those Asian parents of
their life's blood. I wonder if he's disappointed today.

Violence toward our own in Connecticut
is tragedy. The Speaker of the House suggests prayer.
The NRA is silent. In Islamabad or Kabul or any
drone strike arena where, like Newtown, firepower
is no obstacle, the children
and mothers become collateral damage too-
gone in a harsh light and swift wind — that we are willing
to sacrifice for a false sense of security. Certainly

not our children. But whose, which ones? The poet Wendell Berry
demands we name them. We celebrate Bin Laden's death
lament today's massacre and ignore most others.

Evil and apathy
are twins. I want to shake this curse from my body but cannot.
I don't know how. Maybe dance or song or poetry will help.
I only know it clings to my insides like a spiritual stink
a soul decay that will
   not go
   away. ✑

## Pretty Kitty

That first summer was strange and
terrifying in ways I can only
now understand.
Locked wards in a hundred year old mental hospital
are not for the faint-hearted, and luckily I
did not know any better than to apply for
what I imagined was a temporary job — how
wrong I was.

There's nothing like coming out of a locked
door alone on a third floor hallway and
experiencing disorientation and fear
only a novice psych tech can know and feeling
grateful for a stranger with keys, an identifying
factor back then, who could direct me to my destination.
Or taking phone orders from a staff psychiatrist for
blood tests I'd never heard of and realizing after disconnection that
the order was incomprehensible. Calling back for slow clarification
was not my finest hour.

There are many images from that summer —
watching the first man landing on the moon while sitting in a large
dayroom with folks who had seen and heard and
imagined far more bizarre events. Or the older man
named Alfred who in his dementia had soiled himself so
thoroughly that only a shower would suffice. His compliance
and good humor remained as I knelt down to wash
off his legs and feet and his hand found the top of my head and
rubbing gently he said "pretty kitty, pretty kitty." I know
his expression was a blessing and deep appreciation for a humble gift.

It was not my last simple act
through decades of listening
and trying to accept and ease the
consequences of being human
for myself and others in my care.
Suicides were the hardest reminder
that sometimes mental illness is terminal.
I'll never forget the kick-in-the-gut powerlessness
of learning of a young man with schizophrenia
who had just killed himself with
a handgun his parents had given him for Christmas.
Or, thirty years later, the young heroin addict whose depression
  overwhelmed my best efforts.

Maybe that grateful touch is all it took
to keep me showing up, again and again
over the years. ❧

## Falling Down

A man sits at his breakfast table
first cup of coffee not yet cold
and watches as leaves fall down
each it its own unique way.

Some plummet as if tethered to the ground
an elegant falling like Greg Louganis entering water
with hardly a ripple.
Others float on unseen currents as if they may
never find the earth and still possess the
possibility of life.
Many flail about, spiraling & looping
madcap clowns executing circus maneuvers
into the safety net below.

This man finishes his coffee, and wonders
how he will meet the ground at his end.
He'd prefer the diver's style and poise
but suspects he'll be all legs and elbows and
mouth agape confusion
as falling like Icarus into the sea
the absence of a soft landing
dawns on him.

He stands and slides his wooden chair
under the table, hoping again
for the grace
to miss the metaphorical
banana peel lurking in autumn shadows amid
the falling down leaves. ✒

## Dead Santas

They startled me at first, these
flat plastic, red and white
seasonal totems scattered about
surburbia on a mild sunny day in
early December.
They looked like dead Santas
and they were, having not
yet had the breath of life again
breathed into them by a cheerful
homeowner.

As my laughing subsided I
imagined how they would rise
vampire-like, early in the night
to their full height and girth
on the brown winter lawns
ready to delight youngsters and
amuse adults driving by.

And around midnight they'd again lose
their will to stand, not from lack of blood
sinking down to a dormancy
along with the other occupants of their little domain.

A daily resurrection
before the birthday. Now
that's a pretty good trick for
any season. ❧

## White Privilege

Here he sits, wearing khakis and nice leather shoes
as if he belongs or something
coming to our group like
a white savior who thinks he
knows shit about our lives.

White privilege hangs on him
like stale tobacco smoke
that leaves a stink
even in the
fanciest hotel room.

(It's an original sin for which
there's no forgiveness
or absolution and dangles shroud-like
between us.)

He listens with ears clogged by
the wax of history and habit
faintly aware of our language that
leaves a sense of stunned confusion and
defensiveness no amount of awokeness can correct.

I bet he wants something from us, some
fragile acceptance or clue to the location
of a piece of his soul that he lost along
the way in the swamp of place, time and
tradition.

Maybe I'll check him out, ask him
something about himself and see
if he can be real. I'll know he's bullshittin'
if he stammers or looks away or freezes up
like a thief in the headlights of the truth.

He's talking now, with a voice that breaks with intensity
and feeling, telling his story of loss and despair
addiction, irregular sobriety and regret
pausing only to wipe away
his tears.

Damn, this is gonna be harder
than I thought. ✒

## Consequences

Here I am
walking into the waiting room
still carrying a self-conscious brow
after a week
of bandaged healing.

Cancered noses, ears, crowns and chins
all swathed in white, are awaiting
further notice as to where
we go from here
and how we will appear
in the going.

Usually I look away in
the presence of bandages
but not today
as self-consciousness fades.
For this brief time
these are my people.

We carry our wounds openly
if not proudly
for all the world to see
what it is like

these consequences of being human. ⚘

**A Decent Burial**

The history is darkly biblical and too long to detail.
Maybe experienced and industrious Portuguese and
Dutch traders stayed up at night conjuring additional ways
to punish and profit from people
they'd sold in Europe for over a century — or maybe the
attraction of slave labor to exploit the resources
of the New World was just too exciting a prospect
to ignore.

Indians had their Untouchables, so why
not color ours Black — they may have thought. It was an
charming offer to the English, not ones to refuse
lucrative business opportunities. Becoming the
Brahmins of the South appealed in so many ways
as the rice, cotton and indigo plantations flourished and
soaked up the bones and blood of those for whom
race was created.

Hunger, disease, physical torture and random murder
took their toll. Families, broken over generations, endured
beyond the grave and sometimes reunited — but not often.
Lies required for masters to remain supreme were
summoned from science and scripture and digested
as their sharp edges survived in the flow of time
lodging in the souls of everyone, tearing away the fiber of life.

Even a lost war to preserve the "peculiar institution" could
not destroy a gnawing desire for dominance. The Lost Cause myth
and new ways of legal enslavement, some found too drastic
even for Nazis, watered the depravity of those who needed

someone to feel better than. Jovial outings for lynchings and postcards of the burned scapegoats were part of this sacrificial ritual, designed to clarify and preserve everyone's proper place. Each of us is responsible to know, even if we were not eye witnesses.

Hard-fought legislation, to strengthen justice and mercy, set the
stage for political expediency, gradual retrenchment, betrayal and
    erosion of trust,
as those who took an oath to protect and serve, increasingly
acted as judge, jury and executioner
to preserve the order, into the brave new century.
I'm wondering, after all these years, if the multitude of corpses
inside our minds will ever get a decent burial. And whether this
    perverse
social dance around race and caste will go on for
another five hundred years. ❧

*September, 2020*

## *Relationship*

"I am content to walk alone, but to walk in company
with others adds vigor and passion to the journey."
RUMI

**Desire**

Priscilla pulled me through the soft breeze in
a red wagon. Me, at five, on my back
looking up through summer oak leaves
at distant clouds in the bluest sky.
She, at seven, eager to play
and please a younger cousin.

There is a veil between this world
and that one.

I thought that day would
never end. &

**Metamorphosis**

In recent years
    and long since his death
my father has become
    another man, as I have become
a man who sprang both toward
    and away from
him.

I don't know how it happened
    this metamorphosis of self and other.
Maybe it was time
    and the blunting of the barbed-wire
edges of memory, on which change
    sometimes snares itself
and can go no farther.

It wasn't that he became quieter exactly
    or less ornery in memory. Or that I became more outgoing
or boisterous in crowds. Yet we share these furrows
    of the brow that come from life and his maternal line
and ear bristles that defy all efforts at control.
    We are an odor on the pillow, similar whether fresh or only
Saturday bathed.

I see him in my aged friend who
    growing weaker and demented requires
and accepts assistance to sit or stand
    and who smiles from essential recognition
rather than from complexity of thought.
    Like an Escher print, flowing from light
to dark and back again, I arrive where I started.

So time has passed, and now my friend is gone.
    He slipped gracefully into the memory that
changes everything — like this poem picks up
    fleeting images and deposits them
into the stream of time. Like my father and my friend
    I will someday flow into an ocean of memory and
be held only by a few stories
    not long
for this world. ✒

*Relationship*

**Michael**

The clomp of your heavy shoes
on the plain porch boards
penetrates the walls and silence
of this meeting place
like a partly muted bell
announcing the arrival
of a valued messenger
from some distant realm.

We track with our ears your journey
into the warmth of Friends
away from February's chill.
You bring with you a rainbow of color
that clothes your diminutive body
(even in this most somber of winter months)
like a chest full of ribbons
hard-won in the carnival of life.

Black and yellow shirt for bravery
purple around your neck
for loyalty and determination
red baseball cap and sport coat
for humor in the face of adversity
and sunglasses for practicality
and to add a dash of mystery.
You are now the most expressive Quaker in the house.

In the silence, your eyes and subtle body movements
carry on conversation
like a mime conveying the secrets of the universe or
an early mystic in ecstatic prayer.
You make eye contact and peer into our souls

offering the slightly oblique gaze
with which you view the world
as if direct looking might blind us with your radiance.

Stillness is not natural for your body.
It comes between a stomp of your leather-clad foot or
movement to another best seat in the house
like a man searching for the perfect view of some
memorable event for which he's traveled overnight
    through dense fog
or a driving rainstorm
still feeling distracted by his weariness and
the anticipation of the moment.

The end of silence brings you the time to announce
events of your world in words mostly unintelligible
but with meaning unmistakable.
We lean in with ears and hearts attuned
like jazz musicians hearing complex melodies in a steady groove.
With each gesture, inflection, and stomp for emphasis
you say, "I am here. Know me. Take me seriously.
You are important to me. Let me be important to you."

Break-time allows you to indulge a
fondness for black coffee, not too hot,
prepared by friends who count it
a privilege to serve you.
Sweets in moderation bring you joy as you mingle with others
indulging their need for nourishment, like birds who
gather 'round a feeder with members of their species
offering finely tuned greetings and invitations to the ritual dance
    of life.

Later, as the second hour winds down, weariness claims you
like a valued timepiece whose inner movement requires
rewinding by gentle hands in some other favorite place.
This weekly respite from a noisy world is over
for all of us, and you leave with a satisfied
and otherworldly expression
a man whose gift is given in humility
and gratitude, having been granted another opportunity for life.

And each of us is blessed. ❧

## Hand in Hand

It was just the beginning, though
we didn't know it at the time.
After dancing to "Stay" and
other live music as the campus
leaves turned to Autumn gold, we
walked across the brickyard and up a
spiraling internal ramp to the top floor
of a round classroom building that
has not survived university progress.

The large sitting area deserted, our first date going
OK, casual conversation turned to your interest
in palmistry. You took my hand and describe
to this day a peculiar and disquieting feeling without words,
from both the similarity
of our palms and the sense you would know me
for a long time. You did not much like me, and
I was an oblivious Sophomore, simply having a good time with
a beautiful girl who had uncommon curiosities.

Not much else about that night is memorable, aside
from the enjoyment of your company and your need
to be home by ten o'clock, parents' rules and such.
For me there was only one other date with
someone else after that evening.
My attention was drawn back again and again
to the dark haired girl
with the palm fascination. You might say I pursued you because
you were right — we were destined to know each other
a long time and I had my part to play.

Sometimes we smile and think back to that evening
over fifty Falls ago. We might put on that old song
and dance hand in hand
savoring the sweetness of the moment
and feel the lifelines in our palms
wanting our time together to be
"just a little bit longer." ✍

*for Marsha*

## Fourteen Silent Friends

Tinkling flatware music made
on sturdy ceramic plates signals
my gutsoul's receptivity to this moment.
A flavorful smorgasbord
stands prepared
for its silent arc to mouths
unaccustomed to eating without words.
Worship with attention to eating
it might be called.

My eyes make fleeting contact with others
who also search for a comfortable level
of knife-edge knowledge without
the soft focus that words provide.
There is a rhythm to this silent ritual eating
this sharing of life's sustenance
with those who hunger
for deeper nurturance and who
regularly venture to this room
in search of it.
Daylight slips into twilight
and into darkness as my attention
increasingly is drawn to
this circle of Friends and the warmth of food
in my belly.

Pumpkin chiffon brings a smile
with its delicate sweetness.
Moors and Christians, as our Cuban neighbors call
black beans and rice, amiably settle
their differences
with the help of a mild salsa verde.
Pesto islands in the middle of
thin wafers are overwhelmed by a tsunami
of teeth and saliva.
Flavors are mingled
yet rendered more distinct by the silence,
like the faces of the fourteen silent Friends who
share this gathered meal
transcending names and numbers.

And all around the room
these faces dance with pleasure to the
silence that is spoken here. ❧

## Favorite

Like skinny children
of a certain age
playing doctor, we have
a curiosity about
the other.
Show me your masks
and I'll show you
mine.

I'm a stale smelling
variety store of smiles, grimaces
serenity, terror and tenderness.
Behind or in front
which one will I
show you in this moment?
Or which one
chooses me as its witness?

Once, years ago, I put on
an old-man mask in front
of a mirror. And wonders-
I felt fondness for
that moonscaped face.

I want you to take
off your favorite purple mask.
I'll hold it tenderly
and with respect
in my left hand and promise
not to misplace it
or expect that you'll not ask
for its return.

Maybe I'll even hang it
on my wall and privately
marvel at it's shimmering surface
and remember the way
I've seen it
in my dreams.

What do you think? ❧

## Burro

Here I am, feeling kinda shy and cautious
not sure if they'll remember me
even though it's only been a few minutes
since they casually walked away from our little huddle.

They are tall, sleek, long-legged
and chestnut brown. I'm stocky with short legs.
Long ears standing erect add to my height, but not to my
    elegance.
There's more ginger than most in my coarse coat.

I'm strong and sure footed, but never appear in Vogue or other
glossy magazines with a beautiful woman astride
my broad back. My biggest claim to fame was
a supporting role for the sidekick
in a seventeenth century novel.
That chubby Sancho was a hoot all right. And yes, I was there
    in a stable
many years earlier in a story that starred
a baby boy, some shepherds and three admiring foreigners.

Nowadays I hang with the herd and watch for predators
for I am fierce when threatened and stubbornly loyal to
my friends. My voice is discordant — a perpetual nasal
    adolescent
squeakiness masks my capacity for authority when needed.

I have good balance, but don't much care
for running. Those others leave me in the
dust whenever they like, which seems to happen
less often than it used to. Maybe they are learning to like me.

OK here goes. I bet they can hear my
heart pounding as I approach. I tell myself to remember it's
worked before — this reentry to a world of ins
and outs and others. "Hey guys — it's me—
Burro. You can call me bro." ❧

## Banquet of the Heart

I sit at this table of men and
feel a joyous substance
longing to taste the sacred sweetness
of the gift
that awaits.

Humming men's voices reveal
a hive of creativity and nurture
a porous universe of maleness, giving
and receiving
forever unfolding.

What we bring is so small as we stand
before the great need all around us
our measures taken.
I feel tiny and grand in the presence of
these open-faced men.

The eternal questions — what can you do and what
is your calling
fall on receptive souls.
Mine quivers with a sense of hope and regret
and gratitude for this banquet of the heart. ✒

## Mister Lindberg's House

Two old friends and colleagues
Southern women of a certain
refined sensibility
who find joy in runny
poached eggs and buttered scones
sit talking at the breakfast table
in Mr. Lindberg's house.

Seattle's subdued morning light
seeps through the stained glass window,
a three masted schooner
in the arched oak front door.
One might imagine Mr. Lindberg
who was the original owner, sailing
away on that ship
never to return.

Sarah describes first seeing the house
as well built, of solid construction
and well cared for, with elegant interior details.
And she recalls knowing Mr. Lindberg
a bachelor who worked many years
in the men's department
at Nordstrom.

When he died
distant family found Italian tailored suits
hand-made leather shoes
pastel shirts and flowered silk ties.
And it came as no surprise
that the closets in Mr. Lindberg's house
were painted purple, red
and pink. ✺

*for Sarah*

## Something Bad

You look a little funny
and talk kind of strange.
I think I'd better step back
a bit
before something bad
happens.

On the other hand
your eyes are inviting and friendly.
Your body gestures say you may be open
to seeing me
at least while we are still strangers
without names.

So, maybe I can risk
moving closer
at least in my heart
while offering my hand in potential
friendship and learning something about
who you really are

before something bad
happens. ❧

## Thanksgiving Day, 2012

Wind-driven brown
pin oak leaves dance
across the ground of Pullen Park,
white water over mossy stones.
A lone butterfly, living on
borrowed late November time, caresses
multi-colored snapdragons
tenderly
like a reluctant lover
when the time has come
to say goodbye.

Today, the park is lovely with
fall colors and few people
an elegant old lady clad
in earthtones and listening for
the sounds of winter as it
creeps along the edges of bright air.
Noisy Canada geese jockey for handouts
along an undulating black iron railing
bordering the lake where idled
blue paddle boats await the
ice that will bind them until
warmer weather and children's voices
break old winter's spell.

We walk along reflecting on
time and our relationships
with this plot of rolling ground
thankful for our legs and hearts that
brought us here so many years ago

to talk of marriage and a life together. We stumble
across a mysterious memorial with
plastic flowers and broken hearted longing
hidden among the leaves and thorn bushes.

"Will you put me over there in the
holly grove?" you ask. Knowing, icicle fingers play
on my neck and I say "I will if I survive you."
Together we pause and smile and
step back into the gratitude of
our everyday lives on this
Thanksgiving Day. ✄

## Train Ninety-One

The train car gently rocks
as daylight fades.
To my right the March sunset
burnishes gold, crimson, deepest blue-gray
along a horizon punctuated by
Carolina pines in the foreground.

You sit to my left
lost in your book of fiction
inside the gloaming.
Other passengers in the car
talk or sleep or read
as the miles roll on.

Glimpses of flood-lit warehouse fences
slide by in the gathering darkness.
Our train whistles in the background
accompanied by a faint diesel hum.
A toddler giggles
delighted and delighting
feeling its soul mirrored in the eyes
of loved ones.

We are heading South after communing
with thirty-six hundred
psychotherapists.
The thought sounds amusing when voiced
to your shoulder
in the dark.

And to those who would chuckle if they knew
I'd say the world is
all right
here
moving through the night
toward  home on
train ninety-one. ✒

## You Didn't Tell Me Everything

You didn't tell me everything
though I brought you breakfast toast.
You didn't tell me everything
but you told me more than most.

I saw you had your eyes on me
when we passed on Hargett Street.
Back then it wasn't plain to see
I should have beat a fast retreat.

I told you much, but not the rest
while sitting on your couch.
I wanted you to love me best
and not see me as a slouch.

So what I said was sometimes lies
and half-remembered truths.
But never was I acting wise
pretending rich or famous roots.

And when you came into the room
with damp and tousled hair
you took my warm hand off your broom
and led me passed your leather chair.

That night we touched each others parts
both tenderly and in haste.
We laughed and sighed with open hearts
not having precious time to waste.

I loved you best in all the ways
my meager life could give.
But I didn't tell you everything
wanting nothing but to live.

You didn't tell me everything
but you told me more than most.
I didn't tell you everything
'til we finished our buttered toast. ✒

*after Leonard Cohen*

# Family

"Children begin by loving their parents;
after a time they judge them;
rarely, if ever, do they forgive them."
OSCAR WILDE

## Mother's Day, 1999

Today, Mom, is the first Mother's Day of forever
that I will not see you.
Two months have gone since you departed
leaving behind your wastedness and solitude.
Your death brought me deep relief and gratitude
that this long journey is at an end.
Is it only now, I wonder, that the missing
can begin in earnest?
What is Mother's Day without a mother?

I remember
red roses worn in your honor
while noticing white ones
signifying loss
among the seated congregation.
I wondered what it was like to wear white flowers and
maybe now I'll know.

I think back on many years of smiled acceptance
of gifts and cards to honor what you knew
was not your first profession
and your shyness around celebrations of you
never letting on how much you liked
and needed the attention.

Your quiet containment
amidst the whirlwind that was home
left a puzzling void in me
a sense of not quite knowing you.
A deep melancholy, too elusive to name
was part of you
and me.

In those last years
as your body slowly betrayed you
your dignity emerged more starkly
in contrast to the indignity of your surroundings.
Your endurance was notable
a fire so deep that it whispered
in sighs and unexpected utterances
and in your capacity for grace
in the face of desolation.

Before you died
I feared that I might lose the memory of you
from better times.
For this I grieved, and my heart broke with the
powerlessness to save you from your fate.
Yet, your spirit was never broken
not even at the end, as it bid this world
farewell.

You died alone, as I know you wanted
having taken in the kindness
offered at day's end.
A delicious taste of life
a holding of hands more firmly and prolonged
to say goodbye so deeply
that my soul has no doubt of your enduring love.
You left on your terms.
Any accompaniment would have been distraction
from the final business at hand.

And now, for these two months
you are more with me

than for the year before your death.
Sweet memories return
as images of your worn-out shell
fade into nothingness.
Oh, the thankfulness this spring offers
to have known you.

A Mother's Day without you Mom?
No, today my heart is full of fragrant roses
and you. ✒

**Dad**

Yesterday the call finally came
saying you were gone.
Betsy was with you
at the end
and you died calmly and easily
like you always wanted
just slipped away
a thin cloud
passing a quarter moon.

The bones in my body
relax with a sigh
as soft as the sparrow's breath
as she watches a mighty
bird of prey banking away
another bloody meal unnecessary.

A flood of memories too fleeting to grasp
race across my mind
like minnows in the shallows of a farm pond
slippery and luminescent.
And the Hiroshima shadows on my heart
fade to almost nothing
hardly remembering the harsh hand
that etched them there.

It is no coincidence that today
we await, like nervous bridegrooms, the
coming of a hurricane
to the flat, Carolina soil in which you toiled
in early life.

I fear the turbulent, force-of-nature-to-be-reckoned-with
facet of your life might easily be forgotten
in the serenity of your dying
a Beethoven symphony that exits the hall
to the sound of a triangle's tinkle.
Surely, that would be an injustice and
sacrilege to the richness of your existence.

That you'd shrunk with age into a tender
bewildered shadow of your former self in
no way lessens your legacy as a father
husband, friend
a complex man capable of kindness and cruelty
with demons and angels battling
sometimes to a draw, for the right to sit on your shoulder and offer
curses and blessings to the world.

So, tomorrow we honor and claim you
with loving truth
before family and friends
speaking the fullness of your nature
the shadow and the light
inviting and holding the broad stroke of your time on earth
allowing it to touch our lives once more.

We listen for guidance to the sound of crickets
and the earth-rumble of a locomotive in the night
with its cargo intact
heading home. ❧

## Prodigal

This morning, like a prodigal son
I return for the last time to the
old-man mustiness of the house you built.
The weedy grass and overgrown shrubs spring
like loyal sentinels from the earth you so
diligently sculpted and groomed with
hands grown hard and calloused by
years of toil with plow and hammer.

The 2008 taking apart is less laborious for me
than the 1955 putting up was for you. Your
response to the passerby who asked why you
added extra support under the roof when
none of the other builders did the same—"because
I'm building this house for myself and my family" spoke
volumes to your standards and willingness
to go beyond the just acceptable.

Opening the door today, I let out the memories and
ghosts of all of us who, over the years, closed our eyes
under this sturdy roof.
The objects and walls, floors and ceilings lack the
heft or mass I'd grown to expect, much as you
have shrunk with age into a bewildered shadow of your
former, vibrant self.

There will be new owners for this place who
will make it theirs, as once you did. If I return, it will
be as a visitor to take in the new life that
grows here — to marvel at the smell
of creative changes in the wood and stone
and to search for memories that have yet
to form as rewards for
this existence. ✒

## Amen

In church our daddy said Amen
and not some mumbled afterthought
end of blessing kind of thing.
No, this Amen had resonance
to set his voice apart
and punch awake sweet Methodists
like a sneeze or a glorious fart.
Quiet kids waiting for permission
to laugh or pray or sing
were roused to snickered merriment
when Daddy said Amen.

My sister'd chance a look at me
we'd hold a shallow breath.
Our eyes would speak of silent years
of listening til deaf.
We'd track the telltale signs
of Daddy's rising energy
a twitch, a twist, an urgent sigh
a steady rubbing of his knee
or gazing with a fretful look
at an old construction scar
like Blake, just wanting far enough
but going way too far.
We'd know the shame of kindred sin
when Daddy said Amen.

Of all the things our daddy was
he was not a "may I" kind of guy.
Like some large fish in a deep, dark place

beneath an empty sky
he'd gather faith and force a leap
into the milquetoast crowd
and say with gratitude and praise
Amen, Amen out loud.

Our mama she'd look straight ahead
and slip into her place
where Daddy's words and energy
could never sting her grace
or tarnish hard-won dignity
worn bravely on her face.
She'd pray or glance a look around
for her women's circle kin
and feel warm care of loving friends
when Daddy said Amen.

And after it was said and done
our daddy would relax.
As jury, he'd come and heard enough
to judge the sacred facts
and settle back as if to say
"It was near the end of preaching anyway."
He felt guided, calmed and reassured
'cause next week we'd do it all again.
Now he could go and we could breathe
'cause Daddy'd said Amen. ✎

*for Betsy*

## Pants

My father's hunting pants fit me now
though once
he filled them in a way
I thought I never could.

Cotton canvas, Dryback brand
the color of tired Piedmont
clay, with double seat and knees
and a watch pocket.

They hold stains of blood and
unknown substances
and tiny starburst eruptions
marking his journey through
barbed-wire fences that could
not contain small game, or the hunter.

I have a memory of him in a baggy
hunting coat, these pants, shell vest and cap
a cigarette dangling from a half-smile
long before blaze orange was the
fashion or rule and before he quit
the unfiltered Camels.

Blending in, accepting risks as simply
what a man does, the 12-gauge Remington pump
resting easily across his shoulder
making it likely that the night's supper
would be fresh from the woods and field.

These pants no longer hunt, haven't for
decades now, but they remain sturdy and filled
with unspoken history
like the pockets of the departed hunting coat
were once filled with rabbit or squirrel
destined for stew pot and bellies.

He's in these pants as surely as I am.
My belly, backside, legs
penis and scrotum
are held here where his once were,

and both of us are glad. ✎

# *Nature*

"You can cut all the flowers, but you cannot
keep the spring from coming."
PABLO NERUDA

**Winter's Song**

Winter's song is over.
No more sad trombones or saxophones
or frost upon the clover.

Winter's song is gone.
Now come violins and harps that ring
to lead us gaily home.

Winter has two songs to sing.
One is for the death of fall
the other for the birth of spring. ✍

**Morning at Chestnut Ridge**

I lie here, still and waiting
for sleep that will not return.
The sighs and snores and rustlings
of dreams surround me.
This bed is like the warmth left
by a lover who departs
before dawn, leaving a memory
between the sheets that cannot
comfort or replace my longing.

Wild geese summon me to rise and
go into the morning in search of
something that cannot be named.
I want to run or jog
but plod is the truth of
this motion that carries
my body forward.

The air is heavy with scent and
moisture, as yet untouched by the
sun's gentle fingers.
There is a stillness, punctuated by unknown
birds whose voices welcome and guide me in
unintended ways.
I like my body as it warms to the task at hand.

To my left
the dew hangs heavy
on a white rail fence, like diamonds on
the slender fingers of a woman whose
smile beckons from a weathered
doorway in an old
European city.
Cattle behind the fence stare out
with brown eyes unaccustomed to
early morning strangers
moving with jerky strides and
labored breathing.

Somewhere the sun is up and life is
flowing with abandon into its sharp-edged
familiar pattern.
But here, the day continues yawning and stretching
reaching with languid softness for that departed lover, and I
with gratitude
simply receive it. ✒

**Afternoon Poem**

This April afternoon poem
floats down on me like
unseen pollen that I inhale.
It may linger as only
a diffused coughing irritant or
come bursting forth in a
spirited sneeze — all power and sound.
My job is to catch it if I can
and let it take me where
it wants to go.

Eruptive laughter of men storms
across the meadow and
elbows other sounds and images aside, echoing
the bully customer who
breaks in line Monday morning
to be first
for a sausage cheese biscuit
and a
large coffee
at McDonalds.

Liquid chanting floats in between choruses
a bird or two offer contributions
and maybe even crickets. My hearing is not
so acute
anymore.

But the sinuses of my imagination
remain moist and tenderly sensitive
receptive to irritating thought and emotion
and ready to exhale them in poems
to a waiting world. ✑

## Alone

The solitary gull
limps along with legs intact
broken winged
head erect
searching for the flock
that may reject or kill it
hopeful, not knowing of
the fate awaiting it
from earth
or sky. ✒

## December 28

Down by the snow-covered boathouse
wild geese return to the landing
where in a long hour
the ex-hunter will scatter yellow corn
in the shallows. The dark river lies
placid under a low bank of
washboard cloud that stretches
crimson-tongued from the molten southeast to
the north, before breaking into spidery fingers.

A lone crane swoops low, heading
down river and away from the assembly of
hungry geese.
Ducks too timid to risk eating when the man is
present, dive and disappear near the bank, feeding on
nuggets left from the evening before.

Is it the prospect of magnificent winter sun and
golden kernels that draw the geese back at sunrise
each morning? Or do the sun and corn respond to the
call of these geese and do their bidding
in a winter minuet?

I imagine it is a dance set to musical tones
so low, like elephant families talking in the night forests
of Tanzania, that it is felt, not heard, by
all that exists.

My part, then, is to feel warmed by the winter sun and know
that while this moment passes, my life again
has begun. ❧

*for Betsy*

## Flight 270

From above, at thirty thousand feet
white clouds appear
as loose packed new snow.
Morning sun glistens
as it tracks the undulations
flowing west
toward the Rockies.

Slowly, two mounds appear
whiter than the cloudpack
tall and dense and
casting dark shadows
across the surface
silent sentinels
pointing west
toward the Rockies

saying yes — you are headed
in the right direction
toward friends and love and celebration

on Flight 270. ❧

*for Tom and Beverly*

**Patience**

The seabird flying
hard against the wind
ends his journey
where it
began. ✒

**Salt**

Feet in wet sand
moving down
to a darker place
below the
sun.

The smell of brine
and rotting sea life
so pungent in
death.

I think of you
in wet and salty
times. ✍

## Surf

It was a simple thing
entering the ocean to swim
in summer. I'd done it for
decades for fun and now
at over seventy
partly to prove that I still could.

At first the emerald water felt warm and familiar
out beyond the boiling white breakers. Being unable
to touch bottom had been my mark of competence
since learning to swim as a kid. Pools, lakes
rivers, ponds, oceans — these waters had
buoyed and nurtured me
over the years.

That day the water farther out did not feel friendly, more
like a large animal bumping me with its side
to establish authority.
I realized with a start that I was over my head
without knowing how much. Momentary fear, kick and stroke, test,
    no bottom yet.
How many more efforts do I have and
will they be enough to find bottom?
The undulating green creature
just smiled and slid a smooth flank
along my body.

So I swam toward the shore and the family waiting there
drawn by the call of the surf pounding
sandy bottom. Lungs burning, arms and legs aching

this time my feet found grainy salvation
before I lunged forward on hands and knees
propelled by the creature's playful smack.

Catching breath and standing
feeling gratitude for life renewed
acting like it was just another day at the beach as
with the sun on my back, I slowly walked
into the shining warmth
of familiar faces. ✍

**Visitors**

The winter air is achingly crisp as
seven northern visitors announce
their eternal goosiness while
flying low in formation
under a heavy gray sky—
it hangs like the arms of a
weary god, done
for now with Christian revels
this Tuesday after Christmas.

In the near distance
deer hunters bang away in
an effort to re-capture something
that was lost
long before they arrived in the
muddy four-wheeled pickups that
carried them to
the forest's edge.

I've lost something too, but
it's not meant for re-capture just now.
It's meant for remembering and
savoring, like the angle of
December morning light on
a solitary poplar or
the faint odor of woodsmoke that
touches my nostrils
the breath of a feather on
frosty cheeks.

Patience helps
as does an inner assurance that
when the visitors leave
light returns and warmth and
the joy that comes
from having a place on the
never ending, ever renewing
wheel of life. ✍

## Cloud Trees

At a distance the tree limbs
are tipped with gauzy clouds
as if viewed through pale lamplight in
harbor mist.
Often there are one or two clouds per tree
sometimes many more
a random collection along
the park's undulating gravel path.
I smile at the benign glow
and pedal on.

Upon closer inspection these clouds
are webs of dark worms, eating their
ways to a next destination
oblivious to all but the
shrinking green foliage that
satisfies a hunger old as
death, taking them untethered to
another winged place.

My friend says "Yes, they can ruin a tree
these webworms."
And they can.
But in this moment
these cloud trees live
in harmony with their squirming visitors
giving themselves gladly to
a loftier calling. ✒

*for Dan*

**Virus**

The dirt and gravel trail
winds through what once
was Piedmont farmland-
a de-commissioned state road
made inaccessible to automobiles when
the park was created.

Single brown leaves softly crunch
under my bicycle tires or offer
a muted hiss in windblown piles,
like vatted wine grapes welcoming the feet
that carry them toward their
next incarnation.

The virus has not yet made riding in the park
unsafe. Winter air, crisp and inviting
carries no hint of lethality or danger,
not having escaped from other
unknowing lungs onto a receptive medium.
I ride as if this place and experience are
my birthright.

I don't yet know that the world will
be forever changed — that the spaces
I take for granted are ripe for contagion
and death. And that my mind will remain
alert to this danger long after these viral molecules
are gone.

My English friend, already at high risk,
has not yet failed to respond
to my latest email. And I cannot know that the weight
of the waiting will press upon me
like a dozen radiation shields.

Some things are only learnable in the living
of them, day to day. The sound of my bicycle tires
fills up the space in my mind
where, later, fear will reside.

This wine is not yet ready for drinking. ⊷

## Loss and Letting Go

✿

"Heart, who will you cry out to? More and
more alone, you make your way through the
unknowable human beings..."
RANIER MARIA RILKE

"If the only prayer you ever say in your life is
thank you, it will be enough."
MEISTER ECKHART

## Remembering Gregory

At first, it was his height that I noticed
and his curly brown hair
and the graceful way he walked across a room
to greet a friend.

Then it was his steady gaze in conversation
his supple movement in ritual dance circles
the depth of his soulful life observations
and a kind of love that flowed easily outward.

Only later was it the way he moved in water
powerfully, smoothly
as if water was his most natural medium of travel
watching him swim away
a fierce competitor
knowing his admonition to "just have fun" was
mostly sincere.

Next it was his attention to dreams
intense curiosity, adventures in that other nighttime world
populated by shadows
questioning as his sweat flowed from exertion on a bike
or road in this world
holding some fear of saying Yes, while daily embracing life
in so many ways.

Finally, as the stillness came, seeing him taking in loving contact
giving much more than he knew
dulled and sharp, fussy and serene
letting go and holding on
all the consistencies and contradictions of a life
lived in full
coming down to this, whispered through a smile.

"Beautiful, beautiful." ✌

## Remembering Gregory, Again

A year has come and gone
like Gregory, too soon
to fully comprehend
the meaning of its passing.

We feel the missing
each in our own way
and mark the days and months
with memories grown mellow
in the grace of time
and forgiveness.

Have I remembered enough
to hold him close
with the passing of another year
and another?
Maybe not.

But yesterday, just for a moment
the tall figure
moving through a bookstore doorway
was Gregory.

A thought came just as quickly
"I wonder if that man in the black suit
even looks like Gregory."
And he did not.

Yet, the feeling
while tinged with sadness
was sweet
from having met Gregory again
if only for a moment
not in a doorway
but in a still, quiet corner
of my heart. ✍

## Out of Nowhere

I did not see it coming.
The old friend, himself a
survivor of a near-fatal
car crash and a partially debilitating stroke,
said it in passing—"it's leukemia
and if you want to see her you'd
better go soon."

My stomach twisted like
a jaw meeting a left hook.
But unlike Muhammad Ali I could
not shake it off.
Not Frances — who just a few
months ago had a delightful exhibit of her
art and was luminous at age 89.

So, today I went to her home
bearing an Asian card and mixed flowers
not knowing who I'd find there.
The flaxen-haired friend from the past
with whom I'd run and swam, biked and worked
and shared front porch views was now
an old woman in a hospital bed
with oxygen cannulas, looking
very small and scared.

"It came suddenly," she said, "and one
week of hospital chemo was all I could
tolerate." With no cure or meaningful pause
she came home and called Hospice.
"So glad to be home" she said and
her eyes confirmed that truth.
It's hard to remember what either of
us said after that, except a grateful admission
of the good times we'd shared years ago and
the fleeting nature of life and
a small goodbye.

Nearby, her husband looked shaken and
disoriented, anticipating
the awful parting that was soon to come.
He simply shook his head and offered a mournful stare
that spoke volumes. And I, taking his hand for a brief moment
moved toward the door without looking back.

Outside the afternoon sun felt warm and alive.
And my tears met the grass without sound. ✒

**Ray**

He arrived in '29 just ahead of the crash
and became the sixth of nine
by the time his parents stopped  procreation.
His daddy was a textile loom fixer
and inventor who saved money for the company
but not for himself.

He remembers fried dough meals
and being an adult before
knowing about leftovers and
was smart enough in school to attract
assistance to be the first college graduate
in his family.

An older brother flew B-17's in WWII
wrote poems and painted Spanish churches with
courtyards bathed in lamplight.
He was an engineer working for a time
in the Shah's Iran on tasks he declined
to discuss in detail.

He loved his family and felt pain
when his sons traveled a different path after
their parents' divorce.
Ray's inquisitive mind and spirit of generosity
led him to a PhD in psychology and a practice
helping others mostly less fortunate than himself.

So, the love I feel tonight is made sad by
the fading of an old, dear friend and watching his
wife as she loses the love of her life.
The photo of him
in a jaunty hat, with twinkling eyes and engaged countenance
is a reminder of earlier times.
I am powerless to save him
from whatever fate this dementia has in store.

And I will go with him through
what comes the best I can. ✍

*for Donell*

**Memorial Day, 2000**

The nor'easter, not fierce enough
to be called a storm, but powerfully
persistent
pushes tidal river waves into a
foamy skim, like the rising cream in
cold coffee, and moves through the river's wide elbow
below my sister's home.

Blown rain shatters like soft diamonds
on windows that look out across green marsh
to the distant tree line.
Inside the gray stone house
safe, dry and warm I think
of other places and men who
were none of these things.

Places like Gettysburg, Verdun, Normandy
Chosin Reservoir, Khe Sanh, Baghdad, Mosul
bought in blood for reasons understood
and not. The men who watered these gardens
with their young bodies' essence forever lost
the choice to reflect on mortality
open a window or add wood to the fire.

They hover over the earth watching
and waiting to see if we have learned our
lessons from their sacrifices. I fear our inclination
to honor these men will remain rooted in a need
to justify their dying by waving flags and marching
with precision while praising freedom.
The sound of brass bands drowns out their furtive warnings.

And the nor' easter's bluster cannot penetrate
the cozy shell of
my remembering. ✍

**Not Just Any Saturday**

I shall die on a Saturday in April
on a day much like today
when white dogwood blossoms rise and fall on the breeze
like a small boat slowly taking in water
bobbing its submission to the sea.

I shall slowly die after a satisfying and solitary walk
in storm glistened woods or
abruptly while erratically driving through rush hour traffic
with a half-formed thought of you still
hanging somewhere in my mind.

The weight of my dying will not linger except
with a few brave souls who tied their boats to mine.
On this day, not just any Saturday, I will accept
my full portion
of mortality. ✒

*after Vallejo*

## Due Date

Much of my life has been lived
like a renewable grant-
ask politely and make sure
to justify the cost
and it's sure to be renewed.

But lately there are too many
loans coming due. All around me
I see it in the faces of those left behind
when the final payment is made
often shock, always a forlorn aloneness.

I feel it in the absence of certain
smiles, tones of voice, or small boats of
airy laughter that float out from an
amusement park tunnel of love
in the face of irony or artless human mistakes.

In this library of life
the due date is unknown
but not uncertain. Yet, it's easy to forget
how time takes us all, ready or not
into that next open six-gun chamber of fate
to be fired out into the great
unknowable universe.

So, I'll take today as it is offered
these autumn splashes
of yellow, orange, and red and let them
linger on my eye like tart lemon drops on my tongue
knowing that all too soon my
last payment will be made
and this fleeting ledger closed. ❧

## When Is Daddy Coming Home

When is Daddy coming home?
He went to work, and now he's gone.
Before he left he tucked me in
and pulled the sheet up under my chin
and kissed me once on top of my head-
now I'm hearing people say
he's dead.

I heard some cars out in the street
and saw blue lights from my window seat,
and the sound of feet up the wooden stairs
left me feeling awful scared.
The man in blue said Daddy ran a red light
while on the way in the night
to his job at the freight yard.
And the thing in Daddy's hand looked a lot like
a gun, but turned out to be his lunch box instead-
so now he's dead.

Momma's voice was all loud and hurt, she cried
out, saying "y'all killed my man, and a father too.
What's a woman supposed to do?"
When Momma comes into my room, she picks
me up, and holds me close and tight,
and her body shakes as her tears fall down
on top of my head,
where Daddy's kiss still lives.

I'm a boy of four
and don't know how to help Momma more,
except be nice and don't ask too much about Daddy.
'Cause when I do, Momma cries and shakes,
and I lie awake at night
wondering what it will take
to make things right, again. I miss him.

Momma says I'm the man now,
but I don't know how
or even what that means, except
maybe that I don't run red lights
or carry a lunch box,
or I might end up gone and dead
like Daddy. ✖

*June, 2020*

## Southern Speech

How I long for the sound
of a certain Southern speech
a pillowy softness
that belies its content or intent—
the "bless her heart" before the
razor-tongue attack or the
"boy you better not cry" that
sends chills to the marrow.
A rubber hammer can still kill and maim
just more slowly.

In public places the sound has
disappeared, like city fireflies in recent years.
And relatives who taught me
are mostly gone as well
their essence preserved in the
formaldehyde of my memory and
replaced by the sound of invaders
whose swollen ranks
mean no harm, but sound nothing
like my people.

Nowadays the sound I hear floating from
my mouth rings peculiar to the
boy in me who was asked to talk
for family, in Richmond
of all places. They must have
thought I sounded quaint or country.
Over the years I lost
that speech through chameleon imitation
of my changing landscape, more than to shame.

So when that disappearing sound caresses my ear
sun-browned calloused fingers over
black velvet,
even if it comes from a stranger
my heart opens with nostalgia for places and people
and the twilight stillness
of another time. ❧

## Circling the Drain

The comment is offered
as many things are
partly in jest
off-hand, a fleeting backward glance.
Just one of many conversations
in this group of men
all in our 60's
who've met, intentionally
in parts of four decades.

Twice a month
we dine on snacks
and bare our souls
through divorce, spousal death
life threatening illness and trauma
the death of parents — and aging.
We've sailed, rafted, feasted and danced
retreated and charged forward
ever mindful of the precious nature
of what we've created together.

So, the idea and image of circling
the drain of life does not feel
foreign — especially at this age.
Spiraling movement
etching ever smaller circles over time
along with the sense
of increased momentum
carrying us onward.

I'm noticing the distance
to the other side
shrinking
feeling momentary alarm, hearing
that alarm echoed in the voices
of my friends, and simultaneously
feeling calmed and reassured by
the sound of those voices
this shared humanity, this journey
on a well-worn path
leading to the unknown. ✍

*for Gery*

## Chestnut Ridge, 1863

Across a dewy field I yell
through sodden morning fog
"It's get-up time
you boys of mine
there's many a mile to slog."

But the boys don't rise
and all I surmise
as that soggy blanket lifts
are tombstones bold
ashen earth-tongues cold
that swallowed those gray boys in bits.

If I could pull those boys out
of that earthen mouth
could fathers and sons unite?
Could young lovers tryst
in a sweetheart mist
Til dawn had taken the night?

Would they dance and sing
drunken gypsy kings
to a golden July reel?
And would anvils ring with
sweaty blacksmith swings
making shoes from molten steel?

These musings bold
reflect dreams untold
to mother, wife or friend.
Just a weary heart and hungry soul
find legacies left at his end.

Under leaden skies
with wet, downcast eyes I leave
that bloody field
to walk alone with a heart of stone
and little hope to heal.

Those boys of mine are forever gone
like distant smoke from
the last train
home. ✍

## Bearing the Truth

This fading of Ray
is like watching a dying firefly and
it requires me to bear the truth
of his loss.
The effect of his dimming on those
who love him is a bitter herb, even
as his sweetness endures.

The weight in my body is like
wet sand when I sit with Ray
seeing a puzzled expression
where once was
mirth and elfin fire.

I feel the condensing of his spirit
memory and energy into smaller
and smaller space
his life's balloon slowly deflating.
And I miss the depth of
his knowledge
experience and attentiveness.

I bear this truth, speak it
write it and
open my soul to the ache of
a raw encounter
with mortality. 🦋

*for Donell*

## A Thousand Years

On a day to honor warriors
Texas waters carried twelve souls
into the night. A thousand year old
cypress, whose branches gave shade
to Comanche warriors and rest to eagles
for much of its life, was not strong enough
to withstand a millennial flood
and went down
in that deluge.

This cypress, its wood precious
and more exotic and sturdy than most
was turned to lumber
by men with vision who stood
only half as high as its
downed trunk.

A man, our friend, whose voice and fingers
carried souls to a better place was
later washed away in another flood.
He hung on longer than possible, but
time carried him on nonetheless.
Two men, who never met, touched each other
through cypress wood.

Above the lake at Chestnut Ridge
a cypress bench looks out
over time and still water — a thousand year old pew
to hold men not yet born, who will come to
rest in shade on its shoulders. This bench knows
ancestors who passed its way, holds memories of flight
in its folded rings.

We remember our friend and his gifts
with gratitude. A thousand years
may pass again without another like him
to touch our souls.  ✒

*For Gregory Blaine*
*1951–2016*

**Aging or Ageing**

Wikipedia spells it two ways, this
process of becoming older. It takes
a long article with 213 references
to prove that unless
I am a bacteria or a
strawberry plant or in the genus Hydra
I, too, will join all humans and
many animals and fungi as my
life clock runs down
to extinction.

The signs are everywhere,
tentative omens of a seismic change.
It's not just the folds, wrinkles
or blotches on my face or the
brown irregular spots that dot
the back of my hands, mimicking an
aerial photo of some
Pacific island chain.

My arms present their flakey
sun damaged creases peering
up through graying hair like
desert sand dunes shaped by constant
dry winds. And the scrunched, crinkly skin on
my thighs, mocking ripples on a shallow lake,
belies the muscles underneath that
still carry me up bicycled hills, though
not as quickly as in the past and
with greater protest. My drooping
backside or chest may be genetic programming or
just the persistent draw of gravity as it keeps

me tethered to the earth. Alas, my skin just
doesn't cling to the bone like it used to.

I remember as a child viewing elders, who
looked a lot like me now, with a certain puzzled pity
wondering how this happens to people and
believing it would never happen to me. Now
I know both how and that, like other convenient
delusions, this one too has disappeared in a puff of recognition.
No matter the spelling or the number of
councils and commissions that study aging
or the dermatology appointments that temporarily
reshape my skinscape and soothe my vanity
the surety of these changes dawns with a rising frequency
that is stunning. ❧

**Friends**

These friends were with us for a time,
but they left this world too soon.
We knew and loved them in our half-grown adolescence
when life was cool Summer mornings
lazy afternoons
full-moon Saturday nights and
endless possibilities.

Some left us in the spring of life
when youth's blossom still held the
full pallet of their potential.
Others departed in summer's rich
exuberance, with the heat of life overflowing.
Others made their exits in the brilliant-colored fall of life
that, now, all of us can feel
and know that winter's chill
will claim us too
someday.

For now, we share the joy of sweet remembrance
of these friends
and know the sorrow of their absence
from this season
of our lives. ✈

*For Garner High School, Class of '66*

## When It's Time for Me to Go

When it's time for me to go
let me go.

Don't make me a martyr
for a cause that isn't mine.
And leave no place for shrill
steady-gazed voices
unannounced and unwanted
that would enter and defile
this most private sanctuary.

Let your grief fall down
in silence
or in sound big as the sky.
Hold on to those who love you
with arms strong from embracing.
Take comfort there.
You gave me tender treasures
more than you'll ever know.
Now, let me go.

I've already said goodbye.
So let me slide back
into the nightwomb
of mother/father God
from whence I came.
And grind my bones for fish food.
I'll journey sweetly down
into the belly of the earth
and take my solace there.

When it's time for me to go
let me go. ✒

# *Early Times*

## Rush to Oblivion

The red river flows silently toward the moon.
The earth revolves slowly on a silver platter.
I'll give you one, in time, for two.
I know says he who laughs, then runs away.
Time for sale screams the corner vender.

Bulova?

You bet!

A man trips over his own shadow-
Must get that fixed some day soon.
Hey, lets go now and see while we still can.
Winter left without telling why.
So will summer.

Skip, skip while you may.
Tomorrow is for running.
We have mushroom soup in the sky for now.
Ain't life grand said the millionaire.
Great, replied the ghetto garbage rat.
Don't look now. Save it for posterity.

The red river rushes toward the moon.
The earth spins madly on a silver platter.

Ripe?

You bet. ✺

## Sky

I look up.
A sight so real, so vivid fills my eye
  with wonder, awe.

I stare.
Locked in that ever upward gaze
as if focussed on some tiny cloud
a million miles away.

Lost
in the spaceless, timeless arc of blue
  and white and sometimes gray.

An arm uplifted
then a cry.
Yet cloud and sky remain
untouched and undefiled by word or gaze

or longing to be there. &#10086;

## Midnight Rain

Shimmering lamplight falls on wet, glistening streets
of hard, black coldness.
Darkness pierced by beams of gold from a night traveler.
Silence everywhere.
Stillness all around.
The moonless sky spills its sorrow upon a waiting
earth.

Everywhere the sound of smack and splatter.
Dripping eaves give their tears to the ground below.
Moaning wind and biting chill find warm skin
pleasing, but not to be found on a night like this
anywhere.

Rain brings thoughts of past and future.
A time for reflection-
a lake, a beach.
Associations.
Mainly you.

Drops for the awakening earth.
Life's blood and potion,
abundant in March, prayed for in July.
A thing of nature, of the seasons, of God.
It comes to wet and goes to come again.
As with all things.

A muddy drive, oozing hillside,
sloppy tomorrow.
March rain, march.

Twelve bells and all is wet.
Goodnight. ✍

**Back From Beyond**

As I look back, back from beyond
this place seems not half so bad
as it once did before.
But if I could tell 'em just how they will be
in years a few from then
I'd tell them people,

"Look here you folks, you see that time away off up beyond?
Think not of it now, for if you do
when you look back, back from beyond,
the times will have changed and things will seem
not so rosy or so blue.
So for right now, just live right now
have a laugh, a love or two.

Back from beyond is not half so bad
as beyond from back seems to you." ✍

## Earth

Beneath the feet of paupers and kings the bones
    of civilizations lie.
"From dust ye came, to dust returneth" is more
    than just an idle jest.
But while we all must share our mortal
    fate
There remain upon this noble globe on which we
    stand, things which put our imaginations to
    shame.

Need we read a book or compose a verse to be
    attuned to the things around us?
Take a walk along some forest path in spring and
    feel the creative hand of God at work.
Climb a mountain face or ford a stream at sundown-
Life is full, though it seems, the best is always
    hardest.

Remembered best are those beings with whom we
    worked and laughed and loved.
Those with whom we shared this earth and its beauty
    in our time.
That one who gives love and all its joys and asks
    only love in return.
From her body comes warmth for the coldest night
    and heaviest sorrow.

From her lips come light in darkness and calm midst
    the fury of earth tempests.
She has ears for troubles and burning kisses of
    passion for moments of love.
She is always there, but she is not the earth.

For when the earth is no more she will be just as
    warm, as calm, as stormy, and as beautiful as
    a memory.

A memory of earth and time and love. 🖋

## Sea

At dawn the sea appears through the clouds of night.
The slowly pounding, foaming rush of emerald water
    creates the sound of life upon a barren shore.
Our sea remains, though time moves on.
The ages will come to stand upon its brink and
    reason why.

Was not this the way since time immemorial?
No fish or fowl or man witnessed its beginning.
No being perceived the spark of life giving spur
    to its never ending ride through the voids
    of time.
We were not there, but it mattered not to the sea.

Through the aeons powers came and saw and were conquered
    by the onrushing waters.
Not always in some fiery, brimming caldron upon its
    back or beneath it waves
But by the fate to which  all mortal things are
    sealed within this life.
The sea remains while entities and empires are but
    a flicker in the fire of eternity.

Upon the crowded, bustling, noisy beach the sea
    rushes to make its presence known.
It goes unheard, or just unharkened to, amid the
    din of constant laughter and playful moments.
But moments fly, and time erases all evidence of
    the fury of echoing madness along the shore.
Even then, the sea boasts not of its power and
    magnificence, but can it know any other?

Ah, the sea remains to wash across some other
    unheeding shore and with it bring, locked
    in the secret of life,
    eternity's signature. ✺

## From Inside

The making of an inner feeling
was not accomplished in just one day.
Those things we've grown with slowest loving
are those in which we'll always stay.

A tender kind of faithful sharing,
known by far to few,
springs forth in joy from really caring
you for me and me for you.

Your upturned lips with smile or gentle kiss
to say good morning or good night.
Your precious arms, too soon I'll miss
when in a day you fade from sight.

Words you gave in sweet devotion
I'll read, as now, in silent rain.
While from inside this deep emotion
burns precious memories upon my brain.

The small gray bird outside my window sill
sings sweet, sad songs for those above.
But from here inside my lonely being, still
echo your old familiar songs of love.

All songs, once heard, are much the same.
But as I hear them sung again
that bursting feeling without a name
creeps softly on with sad refrain...

to say I love you once again. ❧

**A Christmas Prayer**

When I awake on
Christmas morn
I'll say a prayer of thanks for two
who were born
in Winter.

One in the old year,
one in the new.
The first of these was Jesus
the other one is you. ❧

## What Is Christmas

In this day of war, the bomb, and the darkened door
when the world bows beneath its load of hardships and woe
a season arrives when we must again
ask the question that has puzzled men
    over the wastes of time-
What is Christmas?

Some have said it is a time of reverie, spirit, and tossing troubles
    aside for a moment of careless bliss.
Others suggest the lighted tree of timber or tinsel, and the gay
    presents
        beneath the bows which last but for fleeting moments of
    eternity.
Still the question finds its way to our thoughts and lips-
What is Christmas?

Many others remember the fellowship of the office party or bash
or the vacation received when the day fails to fall on a Saturday
    or Sunday.
But, within each vacationed, tinseled, blissful mind lurks the
    question
        which puzzles all mankind-
What is Christmas?

Still, a few brave voices dare to suggest a meaning quite different
    from all the rest.
They see a tme of sharing, laughing, loving, and living-
of praising some near-forgotten fellow, who never knew aluminum
    trees or plastic angels
A light and promise of life amidst the cold, dim shadows of
    the bare trees and bleak domain.

Who is right? We all fiercely demand to know.
Is it the party, the tinsel, the song, or the fellow
    few folks remember?
From all the rhetoric it's plain to see
Christmas is whatever man
wants it to be.

Yet, surely as this controversial time comes 'round each year
it reveals a light over a darkened door through which we each
    must pass.
Through it we carry only ourselves and our answer to the
    question which is put to us-
What is Christmas? ✎

## Why The Lonely

Why should the lonely have a monopoly on tears?
There are so many other things to give
    comfort in the night.

A heart that longs for only the one who cannot
    come.
A smile just waiting to be given with no thought
    to the consequences.
Ears listening for the voice that will not be
    heard.
Arms that ache with the remembrance of tenderness
    they cannot touch.
A body crying for the softness of its other self
    to drive away the cold.
A soul ever needing the presence of its strength and stay
    to go on.
A memory of times gone by.

The lonely have so much.
The lonely have themselves.

What could go better with tears? ❧

# *Lyrics*

Give Her a Chance to Dance (2012)

Nowhere Left to Fall (2010)

Mean Job Blues (2010)

When You Walked Out (2011)

Odd Goods (2015)

The Beginning of Better (2011)

Ode to Dallas (1985)

Security (2010)

Memories (2014)

Down to Nobody (2015)

Late Show (2020)

La Gare (The Train) (2019)
Music, Title and Verses Two and Three
by Christopher Royce

Territory of The Heart (2019)
Music and Title by Christopher Royce

**Give Her a Chance to Dance**                    copyright 2012

She sauntered in through the door
Made her way to the floor
Didn't give those other fellows a chance.
She looked right at me
And Oh boy, I could see
This lady, she wanted to dance.

So, I gave her a chance
Oh, I gave her a chance
Yes, I gave the girl a chance
To dance.

It didn't take too much time
Wanted her to be mine
But I wasn't talking romance.
As we shook & we rocked
Didn't feel at all shocked
'Cause I knew Rose Mary wanted to dance.

So, I gave her a chance
Oh, I gave her a chance
Yes, I gave her a chance
To dance.

We danced way down the line
She was moving quite fine
And I was sure enjoying myself.
Couldn't stop to explain
Wasn't feeling no pain
So I put all my doubts on the shelf.

At the end of the night
I said "can I hold you tight?"
Thinking that's what she'd hoped in advance.
But then she turned for the door
And left me cold on the floor
She said, "you knew I just wanted to dance."

So, she gave me a chance
Oh, she gave me a chance
But it wasn't a chance for romance.
And I gave her a chance
Oh, I gave her a chance
Yes, I gave the girl a chance to dance.

(Repeat last verse)

## Nowhere Left to Fall

G C D G

For about a thousand years, it seems, my life was filled
   with shattered dreams
And I could find no reason to survive.
All I had was my guitar and a worn out, beat up import car
And a habit that was in full overdrive.

(Chorus)  Am Em D Em, Am Em D D7
   I had nowhere left to fall, nothing else to lose at all,
   Left my virtue and my freedom, and I was gone.
   From the last place I'd called home, took the road and lived alone
   Chose a broken path and a memory, that's all ...

Walked out on my best friends, left them standing in the end
With faded smiles and fists full of regrets.
Battered soul out on the streets, dirty sneakers on my feet
I was moving slow and getting slower yet.

(Chorus)  I had nowhere left to fall ...

I stumbled to my local bar, nothing left but my guitar
That I gladly traded for a final drink.
As I threw down a double Jack, I knew I was never coming back
Blindly sliding down my darkened kitchen sinks.

(Break)

Then your features caught my eye, I saw a choice to live or die
And I haven't doubted my decision yet.
Now you are here within my life, my dearest friend, my love, my wife
Giving me a hundred ways not to forget.

(Final Chorus)  Am Em Dm Em, Am Em D G
    I had nowhere left to fall, nothing else to lose at all
    Left my virtue and my freedom, and I was gone.
    Now I've found a place called home, with you I'm not alone
    You gave me a path to love, that's all.
    You gave me a path to love, that's all.

## Mean Job Blues

E major

This job it wants my body, this job it wants my soul.
This job it wants my body, this job it wants my soul.
This job it won't be happy 'til I'm dead down in a hole.

I'm on my feet all day, I'm crawling on my knees.
I'm on my feet all day, I'm crawling on my knees.
I'm bending over backwards, and there ain't no way to please.

I work for the man, work all night and all day.
I work for the man, work all night and all day.
I'll finish up my working, just 'fore they carry me away.

(Chorus)
> This job it wants my hands.
> This job it wants my eyes.
> This job it wants my legs,
> and it's no big surprise.
> Well, this job it wants my body,
> this job it wants my soul.
> And this job it won't be happy
> til I'm buried down in a hole.

(Break)

Oh, I'm asking pretty mama, for you to take a little time.
I'm asking pretty mama, won't you take a little bit of your time.
Won't you soothe my weary body, won't you ease my troubled mind.

This job might take my body, but it cannot have my soul.
Well, this job might take my body, but it cannot have my soul.
My soul's gonna keep on living, til the fires down in hell grow cold.

## When You Walked Out                    copyright 2011

You loved me best / the moment you / walked out that door.
I tried to be / the kind of man / that you'd live for.
But someone else / had caught your eye
You lied to me / false alibis
You loved me best / the moment you
Walked out that door.

We'd often quarrel / the worst of friends
But you'd come back / and in the end
We'd try our best / to keep our fragile love alive.
Just told ourselves / we could survive
Then some damn way / you would contrive
To leave an icy dagger / buried in my heart.

(Bridge)
I toss and turn / and want you back
But recognize / a painful lack
Of care and comfort / deeply hidden / in your heart.
Now that you've gone / I'm torn apart
But know you'll make / a splendid start
With someone new / who waits for you
Outside that door.

(Break)

There were some times / that I suppose
Our love was good / but heaven knows
We'd lost the flame / in pride and blame
It's time you go.
It's time you go / I know it's true
I'll love someone / but she's not you
I must confess / you loved me best
When you walked / out that door.

## Odd Goods

Just four months out of a big mistake
I was feeling kind of bad
My friend said, girl you better move your butt     G// E7// A7// D7//
So you don't feel quite so sad.                              G// E7// A7// D7/G//
She said I'll tell you just what I'd do
If I was on the run
I'd pack my bags and point my wheels
Toward the land of the midnight sun.

She said I hear there's fifteen guys
For every healthy gal up there
The odds are great you'll find a man
Who will take you everywhere.
I said that sounds like the kind of place
That I've been looking for.
So I left my home and hit the road
With all my dough in a pickle jar.

When I drove into Anchorage
It was about half past three
There were beards and boots in pickup trucks
a 'staring back at me.
Well, at first glance the odds looked good
For this poor soul, by god
But the more I stared the more I saw
By god, these goods looked odd.

(Chorus)
    First the odds looked mighty good my friend
    But then the goods looked mighty odd.    D7// G//
    I couldn't figure out my mind    D7// G//
    Based just on what I got.
    But I knew enough that I could tell
    About this thing somehow.
    If I ever make it out of here
    I'll leave this stage without a bow.

Pretty soon I had me more than enough
Of northern guys and clime
They both could be so very tough
Though some were mighty fine.
They sure had hold to part of me
Felt close to lose my mind
Still, I'd seen enough to point my car
Back south toward Caroline.

Well, the moral to this story
It escapes my mind just now
Though I know if I can take some time
I'll work it out somehow.
But the bottom line for me my friend
As now I finish up this song
If the odds look like a surefire thing
Be sure there's something wrong.

(Chorus)

## The Beginning of Better

It's the beginning of better
I think the worst is behind
My heart's not feeling so lonely
I can sense peace of mind.

I've known pain and betrayal
I've felt shame and abuse
Pulled back from those who love me
Used my life as an excuse.

Sometimes a heart needs a witness
To know it deepest refrain
Now I know my best answers
I'll find time and again.

So for all those who love me
This I tell you tis' true
Your faith has carried me onward
I'll find my way back to you.

(Repeat First Verse)

## Ode to Dallas

The last time I saw Dallas
She didn't even know my name.
She smiled a pretty smile
And I knew that in a while
I was never gonna see her again.

Whenever I first met Dallas
She was alluring as a woman can be
When we held each other close
I understood how other folks
Had fallen for her just like me.

The better I got to know Dallas
The more I loved her tenderly
But every time we parted
I knew that we had started
A thing that would get the best of me. ˙

(Chorus)
> Well, Dallas she is my true love
> I'm sure that she can be yours too
> She's wild and oh so free
> Bright as candles on a tree
> She could love you like she loves me
> Oh, she can love you just like she loves me.

So if you ever chance to meet Dallas
Keep your heart always on a string
Cause if you hand it over
Too late you will discover
A hurt much worse than anything.

(Repeat first verse)

**Security** copyright 2010

Give me a false sense of security
It's the only kind there is.
I need lots of guns and butter
And a double helping of show biz.
Give me a chrome full-body scanner
And a smile that still has fizz.
I need a false sense of security
'Cause that's the only kind there is.

Well my back it aches / my eyes are bad
And my body's not so thin.
My job is in the crapper
'Cause of all that Latin skin.
And Sarah, Karl and Johnny boy
Tell me I must begin
To love this false sense of security
And learn how not to sin.

I know the beltway bums and their elites
Want me to go away.
But, I get help from TV shows
And talk radio every day.
They tell me that my fears are real
Not to listen to what others say
'Cause without a false sense of security
I'll only pay and pay.

Now I know this young Obama guy
Don't look a lot like me.
And the words he spouts with intellect
Insult my family tree.
So, if someone can just tell me
What all this has to do with tea
I'm sure my false sense of security
Will bring me true liberty.

(Repeat first verse)

**Memories**                                        copyright 2014

I've got memories on the tips of my fingers
Of the times we shared pleasures and pain.
When I touch someone new
Hear me say we are through
I know I'll never share true love again.

I think back to the life we created
We had more than our share of distress.
And I thought that our love
Would be blessed from above
But I killed it and gave up the best.

(Refrain — key change)
Sometimes when I'm feeling lonely
Sometimes when I'm feeling most blue
I listen to the tips of my fingers
And I find soothing memories of you.

Oh, these memories on the tips of my fingers
They flood back as the years pass me by.
With each image I find
There's no firm peace of mind
as I dry a love tear from my eye.

(Repeat First verse)

## Down to Nobody

There's a story that I don't like telling
'Bout the years since I said we were through
Lots of women have come, lots of women have gone
Since I left my old life with you.

I know now I was headstrong and foolish
Wanting my love cake and eating it too
Self centered and wild, acting much like a child
I poisoned my chance of a life loving you.

Now I've done my share of rambling
Still searching for love, sweet and true
And I've narrowed it down to nobody
Since I walked away from my life with you.

(Chorus)
>           Oh, I've narrowed it down, I've narrowed it down
>           In my search for someone like you.
>           I've narrowed it down to nobody
>           And she doesn't feel a bit like you.

Oh, it's hard to be happy and carefree
When my bed is empty and cold
I'd give anything, turn back time's fickle clock
To walk hand in hand when we're old.

>           Oh, I've narrowed it down, I've narrowed it down
>           In my search for love tender and true
>           I've narrowed life down to nothing at all
>           Since I left my old life with you.

**Late Show**

She bites off a lot, chews real hard
And sometimes shows up late.
She never tires of fighting fires
And does not hesitate
To tell the truth, to hug a friend
Or challenge pious hate.
Oh, she's seen it all and done a lot
And sometimes shows up late.

I've known this woman all her life
She's my sister and my friend.
We've shared the times both good and bad
And always in the end
She's there to soothe the painful wound
And ready to defend
The least of those among us
On her you can depend.

I value our smiles and good times together
And feel real sadness when I leave.
She then returns to her busy world
Open-heartedness worn on her sleeve.
She offers herself to the hungry crowd
In a way that we can receive
The precious gifts of a loving heart
And a truth that all can believe.

(Repeat first verse)

**La Gare (The Train)**                                    copyright  2019

Here I sit on my final leg toward freedom
Looking out, there are black boots everywhere.
Three men on the station platform, turning
Hunting me like jackals with a hare.

My disguise is not good and thrown together
Women's clothes are old, frumpy and worn.
My losses are great and winnings poor
No elegance on this lonely, cold platform.

Our leader says we must be great again
If only to keep the foes from our friends.
He says there are those who want to take our place
If we don't stop them we may just be erased.

Are these enemies created to keep us in the game?
I get the feeling I'm always being played.
It was all easier when I had no doubt
Is it too late for me to find a safe way out?

They come this way, but maybe not for me
The station is full and it's a little hard to see
Where their eyes go as they search each face
Will I ever escape and be free of this place?

As I get up when my train is called
The tall one stares and I fein a fall.
He walks on by at a fast-clipped pace
And I make my exit to leave this place — forever.

The train door is open just long enough
For me to find my seat and stow my stuff.

As the car moves out, my window reveals
The three men turning on black-booted heels

With frustrated looks on their heavy brows
They seem to know, but don't know how
I'm eluding them and
Making my way to freedom, to freedom.

(Chorus)

> There they stand, and here I am
> There they stand, and here I am
> Just waiting for the northbound train
> To freedom.

(Final Chorus)

> There they stand, and here I am
> There they stand, and here I am
> On the northbound train to freedom
> And I'm gone!

**Territory of the Heart**                              Copyright 2019

{Guitar Intro)

I come to you in morning  /  Walking through the corn
I see your face is shining  /  Through the dewy mist of morn
Laughter fills your eyes  /  And causes me to start
Your beauty is the map that marks   /  The territory of my heart.

I take your hand in mine  /  Our fingers gently twine
Our footsteps going toward  /  What neither of us knows
We hold on tightly spinning  /  For this we've pledged our part
To follow every pathway in  /  The territory of the heart.

Together and apart  /  In our respective lives
In ways that make us expert  /  Inside each others' eyes.
Rushing to the journey  /  Of our masquerading parts
As we explore the pathways in  /  The territory of the heart.

Our laughter and our songs  /  Fill the air with honey sweetness.
Though we know that someday  /  Pain may break our hearts.
For now we choose each other  /  Mindful of the times that fate
May change our passage as we go along  /  This journey of the heart.

{Chorus}
Time may take our laughter  /  Time may take our spark
But while we have each other  /  We'll go on and on and on
And we will go on loving  /  As we have from the start.
And we'll find every pathway in  /  This territory of the heart.

# William W.'s Poems

❧

William W. was a man I met in the early 1970s while working as a social worker in the Forensic Unit (criminal/legal) at Dorothea Dix Hospital. He had been struggling with Schizophrenia since late adolescence, and it was not clear how his mental illness contributed to his legal difficulties and imprisonment. He wrote long, rambling, precisely printed descriptions of events in his and biblical history, and would give them to me for reasons known only to him.

Poems would occasionally appear among these repetitive writings, and I saved some of them for reasons that I no longer recall. I can only guess they appealed to my awareness that, even in the most desperate circumstances, creativity finds a way of expression. William W. died by suicide in prison in 1974. He was 32 years old. I think it is fitting that his simple, but elegant, poems have a wider audience after all these years.

## If We Knew

If I knew you and
you knew me
if both of us
could clearly see
and with an inner
light divine, the meaning
of your heart and mine,
I'm sure that we
would differ less and
clasp our hands in
friendliness.
Our thoughts would
pleasantly agree-
if I knew you
and you knew
me.

## Sail to Paradise

I'm gonna sail to paradise
with the lord.
I cannot fail, so all aboard.
I'm gonna sail around the ice
and dwell in paradise.
I'm gonna live in paradise
with the lord.

## Snowflake

A snowflake seems
to hide
flowers, like songs
inside the heart.

Beneath snows they warm
and perhaps through
storm, they start
to growing.

A song is like
a snowflake
snowing.

## Like Sunshine

A tear will disappear.
A heartache remains.
Tears and heartaches
come and go, like
the clouds with the rains.
Beneath the soil is a seed
and in life's darkest hour
comes the answer to a need
like sunshine to a flower.

*Preambles to Poems*

✿

Each poem was written in a specific time, place,
and life phase; this context is shared here.
Listed alphabetically by title,
this section also serves as an index.

**"A Decent Burial"**                                          *page 31*

The history and impact of slavery on America and the American psyche cannot be overstated. After reading the excellent book Caste, published in 2020 by historian Isabel Wilkerson, this poem flowed out as I tried to reconcile the gulf between the ideals of America's founders and the systems of oppression, injustice, and inequality that have been part of the American experience from the beginning. Her deeply perceptive work is, for me, the best of the recent books that address race, racism, intentional systems of oppression, and the insidious perpetuation of the American version of these systems. Wilkerson takes her reader into the abyss of caste systems while offering a human lifeline that provides the possibility for hope, change, and redemption in our time. It remains unknown if we have the character and will as a nation to address and rectify these democracy-threatening systemic defects. Thankfully, her book offers a more optimistic perspective than the poem.

**"A Thousand Years"**                                        *page 10*

Gregory Blaine was a musician, singer/songwriter, poet, and loyal participant in the annual NC Gathering of Men who died of prostate cancer in 2016 after a long illness. In his honor, a bench made from a 1000 year old cypress tree downed in Houston's 2015 Memorial Day flood was placed on the shore of the lake at Camp Chestnut Ridge, where the Gathering has met for 25 years. Cypress is not susceptible to rot and, like Gregory's spirit, will exist long after all of us are gone.

**"Afternoon Poem"**                                          *page 73*

A variety of workshops are offered at the annual NC Gathering of Men. Lou Lipsitz, a published poet from Chapel Hill, NC, often leads a poetry section. This poem came from one of those outdoor workshops.

**"Aging or Ageing"**                                         *page 111*

There's just no escaping the affects of getting older. The surface of the skin offers, for me, the most obvious signs of nature's toll. And, aches and pains do not assault my vanity nearly as forcefully as the mirror that reflects skin that has been a veritable petri dish of eruptions over the years. So, there is some dignity to be had as I observe that, for now, it remains a rare morning occurrence to feel like I look.

**"Alone"** *page 74*
Watching an injured seagull make its way down a sandy NC beach was inspiration for this poem. For me, the gull carried a sense of foreboding and hope, while realizing that for the gull, it was just another day of survival.

**"Amen"** *page 64*
My father was an intense, religious and cantankerous man who struggled with mood swings much of his adult life. This poem, written after he died in September, 2008, reflects one aspect of his volatile nature and its impact on our family. Recently, a musician friend set the poem to music. I think Daddy would be pleased.

**"Banquet of The Heart"** *page 48*
Each fall, the planning group for the Spring Gathering of Men meets at the NC foothills home of Larry Sorkin to begin re-imagining the event. The combination of masculine creativity, attentiveness, generosity of spirit, good food and rural beauty never fails to inspire recommitment to the process of men's work.

**"Bearing the Truth"** *page 108*
The slow decline and demise of a long-time friend is both painful and disorienting. Ray Collins was a mentor, friend, storyteller and gifted psychotherapist whose friendship helped anchor my world for decades. I miss him.

**"Burro"** *page 46*
A greenway trail on which I ride my bicycle runs adjacent to the NC State University equine facility. On one occasion, I saw a burro

standing away from a group of several horses in the pasture. The poem is a meditation on difference and belonging.

**"Chestnut Ridge, 1863 (from another war)**            *page 106*
Camp Chestnut Ridge, located in rural Orange County, is the location of the annual NC Gathering of Men. During an early morning jog at a time when the US was entering another of its misguided middle Eastern incursions, I imagined what might have happened on the land surrounding the camp during the American Civil War. The tragic aspects of war never change.

**"Circling the Drain"**            *page 104*
A group of male psychotherapists, now numbering four from our original nine, has met twice monthly for thirty-one years for emotional support, encouragement, and fellowship. We talk about our lives and mark the changes, including the death of the man, Gery Sandling, who proposed paying attention to the spiral process, with care.

**"Cloud Trees" for Dan**            *page 83*
During much of the year I regularly bicycle through Umstead State Park for recreation and renewal. On one occasion, while riding with my friend Dan Ryan, we came upon trees with the caterpillars that can decimate early autumn foliage. I was struck by the "other worldly" quality of the images and the enduring cycle of life presented there.

**"Consequences"**            *page 30*
I describe my skin as like a petri dish — it seems to grow everything. Several years ago I had a basal cell carcinoma removed from my brow by a dermatologist using the Mohs procedure. Returning to the surgeon for a check-up a week following the surgery prompted this poem. The surgery site, which initially appeared crater-like, eventually became invisible.

**"Dad"** *page 61*

For the last six months of his life, my father lived in a care facility a short distance from my sister's home in eastern Virginia. His was a complex life, made more so by occasional bouts of bipolar depression or hypomania. By the time of his death, most of my struggles with him were long-finished, and I was able to love him as fully as I was capable and appreciate the legacy he gave me.

**"Dead Santas"** *page 27*

While driving through a suburban Raleigh neighborhood a few weeks before Christmas, I came upon deflated Santa Claus figures on a brown lawn. Immediately, my imagination took off toward what happens to them late at night while they sleep and how they are resurrected each day, only later to return to their deflated state. Both the sight and the poem gave me a much-needed seasonal chuckle.

**"December 28, for Betsy"** *page 75*

My beloved sister lives on the Mattaponi river in eastern Virginia. It is a place where water fowl and other creatures make their rural homes away from the hectic pace of urban life. The silence of the marsh and depth of the night sky are soul reviving. My brother-in-law feeds the wild geese at the beginning and end of each winter day — a blessing for all of us.

**"Desire"** *page 34*

Living in a rural part of eastern North Carolina in the 1950's meant valuing the infrequent opportunities to spend time with other kids. This memory fragment comes from time spent with a distant cousin who, along with her older sister and brother, lived in a large, two-story, white frame house a few miles from my home. There was something magical about their house, with its playrooms, toy closets and record player. I think, for me, there was something magical about my cousin as well.

**"Due Date"** *page 99*

Approaching seventy, I became increasingly aware of friends and family who had died and left others behind to accept and make sense of their passing. The awareness of mortality, others' and my own, was no longer a theoretical matter. Despite my belief that we are part of an endless cycle of birth, life, death and regeneration the loss of family and friends has been shocking, if not surprising. Life goes on.

**"Falling Down"** *page 26*

Reflections on mortality don't come often, but when they do I pay attention. Tibetan Buddhists meditate on and practice their dying over the years. This is done as a way to both accept and enhance that process as well as bring a deep appreciation of life and caring for the living with wisdom, joy and compassion.

**"Favorite"** *page 44*

Many years ago, while visiting my sister at Halloween, I put on a latex "old man mask" and instantly felt an affinity for the person I saw in the mirror before me. It was an odd experience that later got my imagination going as I thought about all the "masks" I've worn in my life and how we know when we are in the presence of our own or someone elses' true self. Maybe those masks are only different aspects of our multi-faceted selves.

**"Flight 270"** *page 76*

In the Fall of 2016, I flew to Idaho to attend the wedding of the son of dear friends who live in Missoula, Montana. I took the image described in the poem as a good omen for the trip, the marriage and the continuing affection for friends I see too infrequently.

**"Fourteen Silent Friends"** *page 42*

Eating without conversation as part of a silent retreat is not an easy endeavor. The desire to share experiences, observations or questions is powerful, especially while eating together with several other participants. The absence of conversation offers the opportunity to discover subtle flavors, textures and colors of the food and observe ones own and others' eating styles — quick, slow, organized or random as they emerge in the attentiveness of the moment.

**"Friends"**                                              *page 113*

On the occasion of my 45th high school reunion, I was asked to write a poem in memory of classmates who had died. The memories that arose and the bitter-sweetness of that remembering helped animate this poem. I've been struck by the number of classmates who died in middle-age (the fall of life) and the escalating frequency of those deaths now that we are into our seventies and approaching our respective winters.

**"Hand in Hand"**                                         *page 40*

Recently it occurred to me that I'd never written about how my wife, Marsha, and I found each other all those years ago. Over the years, we'd occasionally tell the story to anyone who asked about how we met, our first date, and how we eventually fell in love. It's a good story, so I'm happy to record part of it here.

**"Memorial Day, 2000"**                                   *page 96*

Despite the absence of a "world war" for nearly three-quarters of a Century, war remains one of the most evident evils that humans en-act on each other. Our capacity and need as humans to sanctify the sacrifices of the combatants and rationalize the "collateral damage" to civilians remains persistent throughout human culture. So, it is not just for the lost lives that we grieve, but also for the continuing incapacity of our species to create an enduring alternative to war to solve conflicts.

**"Metamorphosis"**                                        *page 35*

I have always been fascinated by the malleable nature of memo-ry — how it changes with time and, even close to the initial experience, can be notoriously unreliable. Memory can sharpen both pain and delight, and it often smooths off the rough edges of experience in a way that allows for new insights and emotional connections. And memory, in the end, is what we have left of life when everything else is gone.

**"Michael"** *page 37*
There is a man in his early fifties, a long-time member and regular attendant of Raleigh Friends Meeting, who lives in a group home for developmentally disabled men. He appreciates the silence of Quaker worship and enjoys being part of pot-lucks, workdays and other social activities. Michael's capacity to express himself verbally is limited, but his body reflects his moods and conveys aspects of his life that transcend words. He is a valued member of our spiritual community, and this poem gets at what that means for us and him.

**"Mister Lindberg's House"** *page 49*
Trips to Seattle to visit our friend Sarah ended when, after over thirty years there, she moved back east. We always enjoyed the lazy morning tea and scones in the subdued light that filtered into her home through clouds or drizzle. The story of Mr. Lindberg's house seemed as subtle and as powerful as Seattle's winter light.

**"Morning at Chestnut Ridge"** *page 71*
The annual NC Gathering of Men meets at rustic Camp Chestnut Ridge in rural Orange County, NC. Early mornings are filled with the sounds, smells, images and anticipation that a large gathering can generate. There was a time when I would rise early to jog, before breakfast with the other men moved us into the togetherness of the Gathering. Something about the place reminds me of my roots in rural Eastern NC, especially the spring mornings when the magic of the day is unfolding.

**"Mother's Day, 1999** *page 58*

My mother was a quiet, busy, loving and steady presence in our home during my childhood — a welcome counterpoint to my father's hypomanic style. She spent the last five years of her life in a nursing care facility where she maintained her dignity as best she could as her physical status deteriorated. I continue to marvel at what I learned from her as a child, as well as what I never learned about her during her lifetime. I wish I'd known her better in adulthood.

**"Not Just Any Saturday" after Vallejo** *page 98*

Poetry workshops at the NC Gathering of Men offer the opportunity to learn about various styles of creating poems as well as to read poetry from various artists. On one occasion poet Lou Lipsitz, the workshop leader, suggested we write in the style of Cesar Vallejo, a Peruvian poet, playwright and journalist who died in Paris in 1938 at age 46. While I don't remember Vallejo's poem, I enjoyed the inspiration and creating in his style.

**"Out of Nowhere"** *page 92*

Frances Taylor Katz was a friend, a couple decades older than I, whom I met when she began work at Wake County Mental Health Center in the late 1970's. Eventually, she moved across the street from my wife and me, and we were neighbors for many years. She loved painting, writing, friendships and the outdoors. Her courage, humor, generosity and creativity were inspiring for me and many others. I still miss her.

**"Pants"** *page 66*

Before camouflage fabric, hunting clothes in the South were designed in browns and butternut to blend in with autumn and winter. My father, due to his loud, gregarious style, rarely blended into most social settings. The woodlands of eastern NC were the exception. He carried his rural, blue-collar heritage with pride despite his dislike for the hard labor that was farming in the 1940's and 50's South. His hunting pants have been as resilient and sturdy as he was.

THE CRACK IN A VOICE

**"Patience"**                                                      *page 77*

This snippet in time illustrates to me the necessity of remaining in the flow of life, sometimes without measurable progress and against all odds of achieving it. Remembering, as with the seabird, a change of wind or attitude may effortlessly carry us along to some unexpected destination.

**"Pretty Kitty"**                                                  *page 24*

My tenure at Dorothea Dix Hospital (1969–78), primarily as a clinical social worker, throughout my 20's was pivotal in my personal maturation, professional development and appreciation for the varieties of the human condition. At the time, I was proud to be part of caring for the most vulnerable of our citizens and the early stages of "de-institutionalization." I now understand, that despite their occasional excesses and abuses, mental health hospitals provided therapeutic communities for patients who are now all too often homeless, or housed in local jails and correctional facilities. Sometimes the losses incurred in the name of progress are born by those least able to carry them. In the case of the chronically mentally ill, I believe this is true today.

**"Prodigal"**                                                      *page 63*

The house I grew up in from age eight until I married at age twenty-two was a brick ranch with a full basement built, aside from the masonry work, by my father. He lived there into his nineties, alone after the death of my mother, and left to live in a care facility only after a fall made it apparent his solitary life was not sustainable. Returning to say a final goodbye to the house following its sale was surreal, with so much life having been lived since I last spent a night there nearly forty years earlier. I felt gratitude for my father's contributions, the ways the house sheltered us for a time, and an awareness that, in the end, it could not and did not shelter us from many of the storms inherent in family life. Closing the door for the final time was a bitter-sweet relief.

**"Profanity/The Curse"**                              *page 22*
American pain, frustration, death toll and legislative paralysis have
only multiplied in the years since the Sandy Hook school massacre.
Political polarization and the profanity of easily available military-
style weapons and magazines have made these events both possible
and likely. Maybe the karma of America's violent past makes this
inevitable. I long for an energized public able to say a resounding
NO to the weapons and attitudes that make the US fertile breeding
ground for gun violence.

**"Ray"**                              *page 94*
Ray Collins was a native son from the foothills of western NC. As
an engineer, PhD psychologist, natural storyteller, beloved friend,
and later in life, cherished husband, he brought a keen intelligence
and humble generosity to the relationships in his life. Watching and
being part of Ray's gradual decline was both painful and frighten-
ing, softened only by the gratitude of having his friendship for many
years and the enduring sweetness of his character which dementia
could not destroy.

**"Refugee"**                              *page 19*
This poem began as a meditation on what it's like for a newcomer
to integrate into an existing community. I realized that the journey
from the womb to the grave is a constant balancing act or tension
between our desire for the new, the different, the exciting, and our
longing for the comfort and safety of the familiar. Finding others
who recognize and value the complexity of this dance is one of life's
most enduring quests.

**"Remembering Gregory"**                              *page 88*
Gregory Burns was an athlete, dancer, deep thinker, and a man
who died of an aggressive brain tumor in the prime of his life. He
was my first close friend to die, and the speed of his decline and
death was disorienting. Often, I wonder about the trajectory of

his life had he lived into older age. And I miss the opportunity to be part of his story.

**"Remembering Gregory, Again"**                          *page 90*
I think it is not uncommon to catch a glimpse of someone and have a momentary incorrect recognition of a friend or family member, especially if that person has recently died. Our mind/brain needs only a few facial or body cues to make a correct identification under normal circumstances. So, when I saw the figure gracefully move through an open doorway I registered Gregory before my mind caught up with my intuition. And, of course, it was OK that it was not whom I imagined. The imagining was the gift.

**"Rifle"**                          *page 17*
Violence has been part of the American experience from the beginning. From the subjugation of Native Americans, perpetuation of slavery, lynchings during Jim Crow, suppression of labor movements and today's disproportionate killing of young African American men by police — violence is as American as Thanksgiving turkey. I believe that for many men, weapons are masculine identity symbols that provide both a false sense of security and fuel heroic fantasies in a time of crumbling gender norms. For me, weapons were part of my rural heritage and, as a adult Quaker, anathema to a non-violent way of life. So, this poem is deeply personal and reflective of my continuing efforts to reconcile often contradictory inclinations.

**"Salt"**                          *page 78*
Beach walks are both sensual and make for a fertile imagination. Who knows where such associations come from? I leave it to the reader to conjure their own connections and images.

**"Shadowman"**                          *page 15*
In pondering the rise and popularity of Donald Trump as he campaigned for the US presidency in early 2016, I heard a woman explain

her appreciation for him by saying, "He says what I think." Having paid attention to the shadow aspect of the human psyche for years, it seemed to me that was part of what passionately stirred both admirers and detractors of this man. Neutrality is rarely a response to Trump's history, statements, energy, or overall behavior. As this poem emerged, there came a point at which the darkness of my own shadow began to bloom on the page, and I had to step back and draw the exercise to a close. My appreciation for Leonard Cohen speaks to both my love of his work and the recognition that spending time in darkness often can prepare us for greater love and light. I can hope that is true in the ongoing drama of this administration. Unfortunately, Cohen's eloquence will likely forever elude me.

## "Silence"                                                         *page 2*

There was a time when Raleigh Friends Meeting sponsored "silent days" for its members and attendees. These days were for contemplation, meditation, worship, reading, eating and fellowship in a context of essential silence that expanded on the silent worship of the weekly Sunday meeting. Silence can be challenging, especially when we are increasingly bombarded with stimuli, chosen and not, and acclimated to the noise of the modern world. So, it is deeply refreshing to have protracted silence which invites the heart to open to perceive and receive the spirit beyond the sound and fury of our lives.

## "Something Bad"                                                   *page 50*

In recent years the levels of fear, mistrust and perception of "otherness" seem rampant in American culture. It is easy to equate difference with threat or menace, especially when we are invited to do this by national leaders who use fear as a motivator for political action. Maybe curiosity is not stronger than fear, but I hope this enduring human/mammalian trait can soften some of the inclination toward isolation or withdrawal where fear is present. Our continued existence may depend on it.

**"Southern Speech"** *page 102*

I was born in a rural part of eastern NC and have lived within fifty miles of that place all my life. With the ascendancy of IBM and other international tech-oriented companies in the Triangle area of the state, newcomers from across the country and world have moved here. Today, few of my closest friends are native North Carolinians. So, it is with mixed feelings that I mourn the loss of familiar sounds and the people who carried them, while welcoming new friends, a diversity of perspectives and the progressive attitudes that newcomers often bring.

**"Stan"** *page 13*

Tenor saxophonist Stan Getz is one of my favorite musicians. While he played in a variety of styles over his lifetime and achieved international fame in the mid-1960's with his Bossa Nova inspired work with Brazilians Joao Gilberto and Antonio Carlos Jobim, it is his wizardry with jazz standards that delights me. Though he battled addiction and romantic indiscretions much of his adult life, Getz found recovery and a measure of serenity in later years. His work with pianist Kenny Barron, recorded in March, 1991 before his death in June of the same year, is some of his best. The compilation, "Getz For Lovers," features his work with many of the great players of his generation — take a listen. You won't be disappointed.

**"Surf"** *page 79*

Maybe part of the male imperative is to develop and test one's physical strength — I know it has been for me. And though I'm not a muscular fellow, rarely has my body let me down in an effort to accomplish a physical task. So, with age has come a reckoning with the gradual decline of my strength and stamina. Nowhere is this more apparent for me than ocean swimming. Accepting limits, respecting forces of nature and still fully living are themes we all face in the last quarter of life.

**"Thanksgiving Day, 2012"**                                    *page 51*
Pullen Park is part of a large parcel of farmland given to the City of
Raleigh in 1887 by Richard Stanhope Pullen to be used specifically as
the first public park in NC and one of the earliest public parks in the
US. Over the years the park was developed with a Dentzel carousel,
picnic shelters, a miniature train, walking paths, a large swimming
pool (originally racially segregated), a children's playground, a lake
with paddle boats and, for many years, a dance pavilion. I learned
to swim as a child in the chill early morning water of the pool and
asked my wife to marry me under the canopy of oaks that popu-
late its grounds. My wife worked as a laborer for the Raleigh Parks
Department building rock retaining walls and implementing major
landscape plantings there in the 1970's. Later, in the early 2000's, she
was instrumental in advocating for the restoration of Raleigh's two
historic carousels and new housing for them. So, it is no surprise
that our walks in Pullen Park are times of reflection on the past, the
future and our place in all of it.

**"The Child Grown Old"**                                    *page 11*
For me, a small-town Southern boy, the 1960's were a time of cu-
riosity, passion, growing awareness and inner conflict. Nowhere
was this more evident than in matters of race. Growing up in the
segregated South, I was not exposed to Black writers or thought
until college. While Black music was an integral part of my ado-
lescence and the civil rights movement was front and center in
the culture, I did not go further and question or explore what was
beneath the headlines or soulful dance rhythms. That is, until
college. Writers like James Baldwin, Langston Hughes, Richard
Wright and Malcolm X spoke to the richness, pain and anger of
the Black experience in American culture that had been all around,
but largely unseen or ignored by me. So, this poem from the late
1960's was part of what rose up in response to my growing aware-
ness and expresses a perspective limited by my age and cultural
experience. It still feels like a pretty good start.

## "The Children"
*page 10*

Among the many gifts I've received from being involved in the Men's Movement since the late 1980's is an appreciation of the importance of fathers. The impact of my own father, the presence or absence of fathers in the lives of clients and friends, and the longing for connection, especially for boys, with a consistent male figure cannot be over-emphasized. Despite the growing reality of single-mother families without an in-house male presence, I believe the impact of absent fathers increasingly affects the health and welfare of children. Over the years, my anger about this phenomenon has waned, and sadness for the children has largely taken its place. Not being a father myself, my appreciation for the role of fathers (and mothers) in the survival of the culture has only grown with the years. All parents deserve our deepest respect.

## "The Crack in a Voice"
*page 4*

Beginning in the late 1980's, men's conferences and retreats have brought me the opportunity to experience male intimacy, creativity, nurturing and  trust. I don't think these things were real for me until then. Exposure to men like Robert Bly, Michael Meade, James Hillman, Tom Daly and innumerable others with whom I've shared these experiences, has allowed me to personally benefit from these gifts and learn how to offer, in small ways, my gifts to other men. An appreciation of men's ways of communication, intimacy and expression through poetry, music and story are added benefits. The exposure to poetry stirred my own creativity in ways for which I'll be forever grateful. This poem reflects images and feelings from experiences at gatherings of men over the years.

## "The Dark"
*page 9*

It's fun to offer a whimsical image and inconsequential idea to the wider world. You're welcome.

**"Time"**                                              *page 8*

Silence and stillness are states of being that often require practice, even for those of us who find them welcome respites from the increasingly hectic pace of 21ˢᵗ Century life. It is amazing how vivid and rich life can be when external movement and sound drop away, sometimes revealing an inner world more interesting than the entertainments and distractions so readily available all around us.

**"Train 91"**                                          *page 53*

The Spring Psychotherapy Networker conference in Washington, DC is a time of communal learning, support and appreciation for the variety of ways we attempt to help others and ourselves deal with the consequences of being human. The conference attracts a large number of clinicians, and I felt privileged and grateful to be in the presence of cutting edge therapists, teachers and researchers in mental health and relationships. Taking the Amtrak to DC was an easy and romantic way to travel, especially when my wife and I went together. This poem reflects our return home after my final Networker conference prior to my retirement.

**"Virus"**                                             *page 84*

The 2020 Covid-19 pandemic raises basic questions about identity, purpose, personal and cultural survival. At this stage, it is not yet clear how the US and the world will be different. But, it is clear that life as we've known it here and abroad will never be the same, and that the notion of "normal" will likely remain elusive for years to come. This poem speaks to a sliver of recognition about this unfolding truth.

**"Visitors"**                                          *page 81*

My sister lives above an oxbow in a river in rural eastern Virginia. There the sounds of nature and small-scale human enterprise are predominant. I welcome my visits, in part, as times to direct my attention to sounds and images that city life no longer offers. Canada geese are frequent visitors and bring their unique voices and familiar rhythms to the river's ever-changing atmosphere. Hunters mark the year's cycles with their winter voyages in search of deer and comradeship. Sometimes, both are elusive.

**"What Would Rumi Say?"** *page 7*

The first Gulf War was disturbing on many levels, not the least of which was the destruction wrought on the Iraqi's by the US's superior air and ground forces. The war seemed arbitrary in the extreme and a missed opportunity to exercise diplomatic muscle rather than demonstrate US military might. At the time, I was becoming increasingly familiar with the poetry of Jalaluddin Rumi. I easily imagined the distress such a conflict would bring to someone like Rumi who, though he was Persian and born in what is now Afghanistan, was immersed in that part of the world and was capable of eloquent descriptions of the human condition.

**"When Is Daddy Coming Home"** *page 100*

The disproportionate killing of young, Black men by police in the US has been well-documented for many years. Yet, it is only in the midst of the 2020 Covid-19 pandemic that the killings have sparked sustained resistance by both communities of color and white allies. Systemic racism is being identified and attacked for its lethality and trans-generational support of white supremacy. This poem gets at the personal cost for a son of the loss of a father at the hands of those whose mission has been to "protect and serve."

**"When It's Time For Me To Go"** *page 114*

In 1990 a young woman named Terri Schiavo suffered cardiac arrest, was resuscitated, but subsequently entered a persistent vegetative state due to lack of oxygen to her brain. Eventually the efforts of her husband/guardian to withdraw life support according to her wishes and her parents' efforts to prevent this became a medical/political drama that played out until 2005. Terri Schiavo became a cause celebre for disability rights and right-to-die advocates, as well as politicians who saw the potential for political gain by joining the fray. During this time, a woman with disabilities made an impassioned statement in Raleigh Friends Meeting decrying efforts to allow Ms Schiavo to die and encouraging preservation of her life at any cost. This poem came from my recognition that there are worse things than dying, one of which would be being prevented from dying when my time has come. This poem honors Terri Schiavo's life and death.

**"White Privilege"**                                                    *page 28*

The construct of "race" has been part of American society from the beginning. In recent years racism has taken on more subtle, and some say more insidious, forms within a system that still struggles with issues of justice, civil rights, and social equality for people of color. This poem came from my continuing efforts to accept how the privileges of whiteness permeate my thinking and behavior in everyday life. And, it is an effort to remember that human suffering knows no color, class or status and cannot be measured by the balance in one's bank account.

**"Winter's Song"**                                                      *page 70*

I have no idea where this poem came from or when I wrote it. The original, which I recently discovered while searching an old journal, is written in pencil on yellowing, five-hole notebook paper with corrections and has no date. Several years ago my sister gave me a framed copy of it accompanied by some of her watercolor plant drawings. I still like the simplicity of the words and images and usually recite it in Raleigh Friends Meeting to welcome spring.

**"You Didn't Tell Me Everything"**                                      *page 55*

My friend Richard Kevin re-introduced me to the music & poetry of Leonard Cohen (d. 2016) several years ago and recently gifted me with Cohen's final work, "The Flame," a volume of poems, notebooks, lyrics and drawings published in 2018. Cohen's capacity to explore the sacred and profane, the light and shadow of human experience, and the melodic dance of relationship was remarkable. This recent poem was inspired by reading from Cohen's last work, as well as the humble example of the humanity he gave the world to the end of his life. Thanks, Leonard.

## "Early Times" Section

These poems, like "The Child Grown Old," come from the time prior to my graduation from NCSU in May, 1970 at age 22. Some of them obviously were inspired by my relationship with my future wife Marsha, who was my muse in many ways, including the opening of my heart to intense emotions and my eyes to social/cultural issues. The poem "What Is Christmas" was a gift to Marsha for our first shared Christmas in 1967, only a few months after our initial meeting.

They reflect a growing awareness of life that college in the late 1960's offered a young man who came from a religious family in a small, Southern town. The swirl of emotions, ideas, questions and longings came bubbling out in response to the times and the people who challenged my preconceived notions and gave me permission and invitation to pay attention. Living at home and commuting to NCSU insulated me from some of the distractions of college life and allowed for a more solitary existence prior to meeting Marsha in the fall of 1967. My religious/spiritual life, while still based in rather traditional Christianity, began to mature and include elements of what has been called the "social gospel" with emphasis on war and civil rights. And my night work at Dorothea Dix Hospital as a psychiatric healthcare technician during my final year at NCSU gave me a much broader sense of human experience and applied psychological understanding.

So, while most of these poems are not attributable to specific images or experiences, collectively they reflect a questioning, observing, and sensing self that was growing and changing during what I now understand as my late adolescence. And while they reflect a beginner's technique, there are glimmers of phrases or descriptions that would emerge in later years in a more mature, informed fashion. I offer them in the form in which they have existed for over fifty years.

## About the Author

Doug Jennette is a native North Carolinian who, over the years, has written in an occasional and inspirational fashion. His poems flow from encounters with intense emotions, vivid images in nature, or people who evoke words or phrases that interest him, and ultimately give him courage to live a better life. His career as a psychotherapist and his lengthy involvement in men's work informs and shapes his appreciation of the human longing for intimate connection, beauty, and the grief that is part of every life. Doug is retired and lives in Raleigh, NC with his wife of fifty years, Marsha.

1964 ~~Passing~~

First ~~dawning~~ of the ~~fairliest~~ days
a little while ~~from~~ Spring
Winter's ~~song~~

Winter's song is over.
No more sad trombone ~~and~~ and saxophone
And ~~frost~~ upon the clover.

~~———~~

Winter's song is gone.
~~Harps of spring~~
~~Refrain~~ Now come violins and ~~harps of spring~~ that ring
~~and~~ lead us gaily home.

Winter has two songs to sing.
One is for the death of Fall,
The other for the birth of Spring.

D. Jennette

CPSIA information can be obtained
at www.ICGtesting.com
Printed in the USA
LVHW021930180121
676816LV00015B/126

9 780578 814407